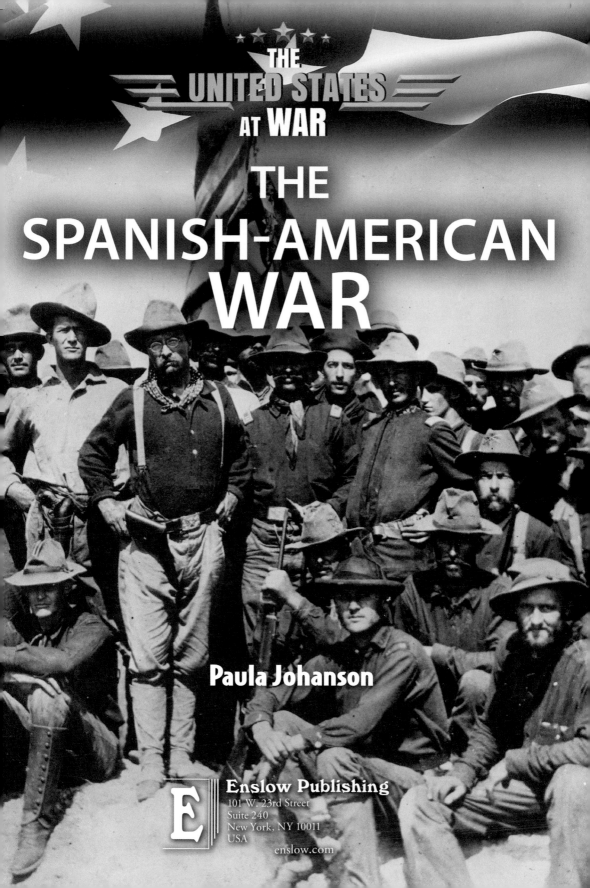

THE UNITED STATES AT WAR

THE SPANISH-AMERICAN WAR

Paula Johanson

Enslow Publishing

101 W. 23rd Street
Suite 240
New York, NY 10011
USA

enslow.com

Published in 2017 by Enslow Publishing, LLC.
101 W. 23rd Street, Suite 240, New York, NY 10011

Library of Congress Cataloging-in-Publication Data
Names: Johanson, Paula.
Title: The Spanish-American War / Paula Johanson.
Description: New York, NY : Enslow Publishing, 2017. | Series: The United States at war
| Includes bibliographical references and index.
Identifiers: LCCN 2016005248 | ISBN 9780766076655 (library bound)
Subjects: LCSH: Spanish-American War, 1898—Juvenile literature.
Classification: LCC E715 .J72 2017 | DDC 973.8/9—dc23
LC record available at http://lccn.loc.gov/2016005248

Printed in the United States of America

To Our Readers: We have done our best to make sure all websites in this book were
active and appropriate when we went to press. However, the author and the
publisher have no control over and assume no liability for the material available on
those websites or on any websites they may link to. Any comments or suggestions can
be sent by e-mail to customerservice@enslow.com.

Portions of this book originally appeared in the book T*he Spanish-American War:
"Remember the Maine!"* by Robert Somerlott.

Photo Credits: Cover, p.1 Memory Stockphoto/Shutterstock.com (insignia), Sergey
Kamshylin/Shutterstock.com (US flag); William Dinwiddie/Hulton Archive/Getty Images;
pp. 4–5 Everett Historical/Shutterstock.com; pp. 6, 8, 15, 18, 22, 24, 37, 50, 56, 60, 94,
125 Library of Congress; p. 12 Public Domain/British Library HMNTS 9771.de.15/
File:Captain Charles Dwight Sigsbee.jpg/Wikimedia Commons; p. 20 PHAS/UIG/Getty
Images; pp. 26, 32, 98 © North Wind Picture Archives; p. 40 Culture Club/Hulton
Archive/Getty Images; p. 44 Print Collector/Hulton Archive/Getty Images; p. 45
File:Richard R Wright.jpg/Wikipedia; p. 48 Interim Archives/Getty Images; p. 63 James
Burton/File:How the Rough Riders rode to Port Tampa, 1898.jpg/Wikimedia Commons;
p. 68 Historical Art Collection (HAC)/Alamy Stock Photo; p. 70 Heritage Image
Partnership Ltd/Alamy Stock Photo; p. 79 Classic Image/Alamy Stock Photo; p. 84 US
Army/National Archives/The LIFE Picture Collection/Getty Images; p. 86 Niday Picture
Library/Alamy Stock Photo; p. 88 Wyllie, William Lionel/Private Collection/©Look and
Learn/Illustrated Papers Collection/Bridgeman Images; p. 100 Peter Hermes Furian/
iStock/Thinkstock; p. 103 Universal History Archive/Getty Images; p. 108 Print Collector/
Print Collector/Getty Images; p. 110 Public Domain/Frances Benjamin Johnston/File:Jules
Cambon signs Treaty of Paris, 1899.JPG/Wikimedia Commons; p. 116 Universal History
Archive/UIG via Getty Images; p. 123 Hulton Archive/Getty Images.

CONTENTS

FOREWORD

Four weeks after *USS Maine* sank in Cuba's Havana Harbor and four weeks before war with Spain was declared, Senator Redfield Proctor of Vermont addressed the US Senate. In Proctor's speech, he described the horrid conditions he had witnessed visiting Cuba under Spanish rule. In particular, he focused on the effects of Captain-General Valeriano Weyler's reconcentration policy. This program drove Cuban civilians into fortified towns in order to restrict movement of rebels fighting for Cuban independence. In these concentration camps, it was difficult to grow food or maintain communities. For two years, Spanish restriction of the Cuban population and their cattle and food led to disease and starvation. The following excerpt is from the speech given by this Republican senator on March 17, 1898:

It is not within the narrow limits of my vocabulary to portray it. I went to Cuba with a strong conviction that the picture had been overdrawn; that a few cases of starvation and suffering had inspired and stimulated the press correspondents, and that they had given free play to a strong, natural and highly cultivated imagination.

I could not believe that out of a population of one million six hundred thousand, 200,000 had died within these Spanish forts, practically prison walls, within a few months past, from actual starvation and disease caused by insufficient and improper food.

My inquiries were entirely outside of sensational sources. They were made by our medical officers, of our consuls, of city alcaldes [mayors], of relief committees, of leading merchants and bankers, physicians and lawyers. Several of my informants were Spanish born, but every time came the answer that the case had not been overstated.

What I saw I cannot tell so that others can see it. It must be seen with one's own eyes to be realized.

There are many things worse than war. It may be that the United States is to become the Knight Errant of the world. War with Spain may put her in a position to demand civil and religious liberty for the oppressed of every nation and of every clime.

—Methodist bishop Charles C. McCabe at the onset of the Spanish-American War

HAVANA HARBOR EXPLOSION

"THERE ARE MANY THINGS WORSE THAN WAR. IT MAY BE THAT THE UNITED STATES IS TO BECOME THE KNIGHT ERRANT OF THE WORLD. WAR WITH SPAIN MAY PUT HER IN A POSITION TO DEMAND CIVIL AND RELIGIOUS LIBERTY FOR THE OPPRESSED OF EVERY NATION AND EVERY CLIME."

— Methodist bishop Charles C. McCabe at the onsert of the Spanish-American War.

On February 15, 1898, the battleship USS *Maine* was anchored in the harbor of Havana, Cuba. This was the Maine's first time in Havana, and the first time an American naval vessel had visited Cuba in three years. The 354-foot-long (108-m) ship had 355 American sailors for crew. Most of the men and officers were below-decks and off-duty, while the few men on guard duty patrolled the decks, tense in the shadow of Moro Castle. The ship's magazines were full of ammunition, and on the gun deck near the one- and six-pound guns were many boxes of shells.

This photo shows the USS Maine *when it entered Havana Harbor.*

Captain Charles S. Sigsbee, who had sailed the *Maine* into Havana Harbor two weeks before, felt he had been sent on a risky mission. He had "sensed danger" and taken precautions. His ship was ready for quick action.[1] Yet tonight there was not the least sign of trouble. Nothing disturbed the quiet harbor.

At nine o'clock the ship's bell rang the hour. The *Maine's* bugler played "Taps"—the final bugle command of the day and the signal for "lights out." As it turned out, this bugle call would be the last ever to be sounded on the deck of the American ship.

The air was a bit hazy that evening. Captain Sigsbee noticed that the thin mist was interrupted by bright tropical star constellations.[2] Despite the haze, he would see clearly if any suspicious boats approached the *Maine.*

Captain Sigsbee could make out the forbidding stone tower of Moro Castle, dark against the sky, across the bay. The castle, built long ago to defend Havana against pirates or other invaders, loomed as a symbol of the once-mighty power of Spain. Once, Spain had boasted the greatest empire in the world, controlling most of Central and South America. Some former Spanish colonies—Mexico, Argentina, Peru, and a dozen other Latin American countries—had become independent nations. Cuba still remained under Spanish control, but the island was struggling—without success so far—to gain its freedom.

In 1895, after decades of futile revolt, a simmering Cuba erupted into a full-scale war for independence. Spanish reaction was swift and brutal. Lines of blockhouses, which are small, easily-defended buildings, and barbed wire fences were built across the narrow parts of the island. Most of the farming population, consisting of thousands of civilians, was held in detention camps as Cuba bristled with bayonets and violence. On the island, killings and starvation were rampant.

A weakened Spain had lost many of its vast possessions, but some islands—including the Philippines and Puerto Rico—were still held by the Spanish Crown. A large area in North Africa also remained under Spain's control.

Cuba, Spain's oldest, large colony in the New World, was still its proudest possession. Centuries ago, Spanish invaders had launched their great conquests from Cuba, seizing Mexico, Central America, and most of the huge South American continent as well.

The damp stone dungeons of Moro Castle had once held rebels and traitors against Spain, who were brought to Havana for punishment. There was a torture chamber, which housed a heavy chair used to hold prisoners being executed. The castle fortress remained a terrifying place to anyone who resisted Spanish rule.

If Moro Castle was a symbol of ancient Spanish power, then the *Maine* reflected the military force of the modern United States. In its hold were torpedoes, and the ship was loaded with artillery, including guns powerful enough to blast down the whole Havana waterfront. One officer, boasting of the ship's weapons, once said, "We have Havana at our mercy."[3]

The *Maine* had been sent to Cuba to display American military power. Its official mission was to protect the lives and property of American citizens in Cuba. If the violent revolution in the island's countryside should spill over into Havana, Captain Sigsbee and his men stood ready to intervene and evacuate any Americans in danger. So far, the Cuban capital seemed quiet and safe, and Spanish officials privately ridiculed the American fears of riots in Havana, resenting the presence of a foreign battleship in their harbor.

Cuba lies only ninety miles (145 km) from Florida, making it one of America's closest neighbors. For months, a segment of the people in the United States had been angrily protesting Spain's treatment of the Cuban people during their struggle for independence. Horror stories appeared in American newspapers: accounts of torture, murder, and starvation. Some of these reports had been exaggerated, but others were all too true. An investigator sent to Cuba by the U.S. government claimed that a full third of the rural population of Cuba had already died as the result of war, imprisonment, and starvation.[4]

William McKinley, president of the United States, hoped that American outrage would not lead to actual war—at least not yet. He claimed America should not be "plunged into war until we are ready for it."[5] McKinley also said that if he could avoid war, he would be the happiest man in the world. He had already seen too much bloodshed in the American Civil War. The president's words rejecting war, however, also seemed to suggest that war was very possible. Sending the battleship *Maine* to Havana was a strong warning to the Spaniards that the United States cared deeply about the inhumane events taking place so close to its border.

Captain Sigsbee felt no alarm as he stood at the railing of the *Maine* for what would be the last time and listened to some crewman playing a mandolin in the darkness of the ship.[6] He also heard distant music that night. Along the Havana waterfront stood outdoor cafés where people gathered in the evening for supper, to drink, or to chat. If they were lucky, they also enjoyed a cooling night breeze from the sea. Captain Sigsbee could see twinkling lights near these café tables as music floated softly across the dark water.[7]

Captain Sigssbee is best remembered as captain of the Maine, *but he served in many naval engagements during the Civil War and would have a long career after the Spanish-American War as well.*

Investigative Journalists

On Havana's waterfront, two American journalists, who were becoming famous in Cuba, were seated at a café table. George Bronson Rea wrote about Cuba for the *New York Herald*. His companion, Sylvester Scovel, was a reporter for another New York newspaper, the *World*. Both men had traveled extensively throughout Cuba. Likewise, both had watched recent events closely and talked to countless Cuban people. Yet, despite their similar experiences, they had reached very different conclusions regarding Cuba's current conditions.

Rea believed that American newspapers were printing lies to boost their circulation, and trying to "embroil the U.S. in a war with Spain."[8] He was especially angry about accounts that the Spanish authorities had been "feeding Cuban prisoners to the sharks" near Moro Castle. "It never happened," he said, pronouncing such reports "rot."[9] In Rea's view, "too much sympathy has been wasted on the Cuban rebellion."[10] The reporter blamed both sides for crimes that had been committed and described General Máximo Gómez, the leader of the rebels, as "a withered old man who gave one the idea of a resurrected Egyptian mummy."[11] Scovel believed almost the opposite. He declared: "Extermination of the Cuban people under the cloak of civilized warfare is Spain's settled purpose."[12]

While in Cuba, the two men had shared many dangerous and life-threatening experiences in the mountains and jungles. They had become friends, and tonight, as they sat looking at the quiet harbor, they could clearly see the *Maine* at anchor in the distance. No boats were approaching the vessel, and it did not worry the reporters that armed American sailors were pacing the decks.

A few minutes later, a terrible explosion shattered the night. The windows of the café were blown out, spraying the reporters with broken glass. Running into the waterfront street, they saw flames rising from where they had earlier seen the *Maine*. Scovel later wrote that "the harbor was lit up with intense light and above it could be seen innumerable colored lights resembling rockets."[13]

Red Cross Founder in Havana

One of America's most admired women was in Havana that night, working where she had a clear view of the harbor. This woman was Clara Barton, the founder of the American Red Cross and the great reformer of military hospitals. She had gained fame during the Civil War.

Barton had studied the U.S. government report describing the starvation, poverty, and lack of medical care in Cuba. This pushed her into action, sending Barton directly to the White House to see the president. McKinley named her as head of a volunteer committee to aid the Cubans.

Six months later, Barton and a Spanish translator arrived in Havana with food and medical supplies. Barton found the Spanish officials polite but unhelpful as she inspected hospital conditions and sought bakers to help turn flour into bread.

At this time, the Spanish government had imprisoned thousands of Cubans with suspected rebel sympathies in concentration camps. These prisoners faced starvation, and Clara Barton begged the Havana authorities to allow the captives to plant crops inside the fences that confined them. The Spaniards listened to her with grave sympathy, nodded, and did nothing.[14]

What Clara Barton found in Cuba horrified her. She saw starvation and suffering all around her. She had never seen such cruelty as she discovered in Cuba, and it seemed to her that the Spanish government was to blame.

Now another of Barton's long days of work was ending. She looked out at the harbor and saw the *Maine* standing at anchor in the calm water. Barton was finishing up when a terrible explosion shook the windows.

Clara Barton was called the Angel of the Battlefield during the Civil War.

Barton later wrote, "The deafening roar was a burst of thunder as perhaps one never heard before. And off to the right, out over the bay, the air was filled with a blaze of light."[15]

Two Explosions

Aboard the *Maine*, Captain Sigsbee had heard the three chimes that signaled nine-thirty. He spent the next ten minutes finishing a letter to his wife. Just as he had folded the page and was putting it into an envelope, a blast rocked the ship.

There were two explosions, one rapidly after the other. Within a second or two, a rain of objects fell from overhead: fragments of steel railings, lumps of cement, blocks of wood. Some of the crew were knocked down and injured by the flying debris. Others never awoke in their bunk beds and hammocks, killed by the blast as they slept. Some ran toward the deck to take battle stations or to begin launching boats, as the ship was rapidly sinking.

Captain Sigsbee, the letter to his wife still in his hand, heard "a bursting, rending, crashing roar of immense volume."[16] He felt the ship lurch and tip. All lights went out and smoke poured into his cabin. As Sigsbee struggled in the darkness, the ship tilted sharply and the captain had to crawl through a porthole to reach the main deck. A sailor described him standing there calmly, "as cool as if at a ball."[17]

Captain Sigsbee, not knowing what might happen next, shouted to the crew to prepare to ward off any hostile boarders attempting to get onto the *Maine*. He then realized that there was almost no one left to obey the order and actually not much left to protect. The *Maine* was a hopeless wreck.

Sigsbee believed his ship had been mysteriously attacked. Perhaps a torpedo had struck it; perhaps some fort on shore had fired a cannon. He could not, at the time, explain it.

Parts of the ship had burst into flame. By the light of the fires, Sigsbee could see that the *Maine* had already become a twisted mass of metal. As he splashed through the water rapidly rising on the deck, Sigsbee believed he heard cheers on the distant shore.[18] He then ordered the few remaining lifeboats quickly lowered to rescue the "white forms" of sailors, whether living or dead, from the dark waters of Havana harbor.

By this time, reporters Scovel and Rea had found a boat and were rowing toward the sinking ship. When they approached the area of the explosion, Rea described the scene: "The bow had disappeared. The foremast and smokestacks had fallen, and to add to the horror, the mass of wreckage amidships was on fire."[19]

Clara Barton wasted no time looking at the harbor. She hurried to the large Havana hospital, San Ambrosio, where "thirty to forty" of the wounded *Maine* sailors had been taken. "They had been crushed by timbers, cut by iron, scorched by fire."[20] Since the Spanish doctors seemed to have the terrible scene under control, Barton began to take down the names and addresses of the wounded sailors. Most of the victims were either already dead or were on the verge of dying. She wanted to let their families know what had happened to them.

News by Telegraph

In the wake of the disaster, Spanish authorities halted telegraph messages from Havana. Reporter Scovel, who had stolen a blank cable, managed to get about a hundred words to the Associated

This engraving shows the destruction of the USS Maine. Sailors are being thrown into the harbor by the blast.

Press, a company that gathers news for many American newspapers. The first solid news came from a Cuban agent working secretly for American naval intelligence in Havana. Soon after ten o'clock in Key West, Florida, the telegraph receiver began clicking, alerting Americans that the *Maine* had been sunk.

No one could quite believe this first report, but then a clear message came in from Captain Sigsbee: "*Maine* blown up in Havana harbor at nine forty tonight and destroyed. Many wounded and doubtless more killed or drowned."[21]

"This Means War"

About two hours later in New York City, William Randolph Hearst, owner and publisher of the *New York Journal*, received a message about the explosion in Havana. For months, Hearst had been printing horror stories, both true and false, about events in Cuba. Often, he had been accused of promoting an armed struggle between Spain and the United States. Now, he asked the night editor what would be on the front page of their newspaper besides articles about the *Maine* explosion.

"Only the other big news," replied the editor.

"There is not any other big news," said Hearst. "Please spread the story all over the page. This means war!"[22]

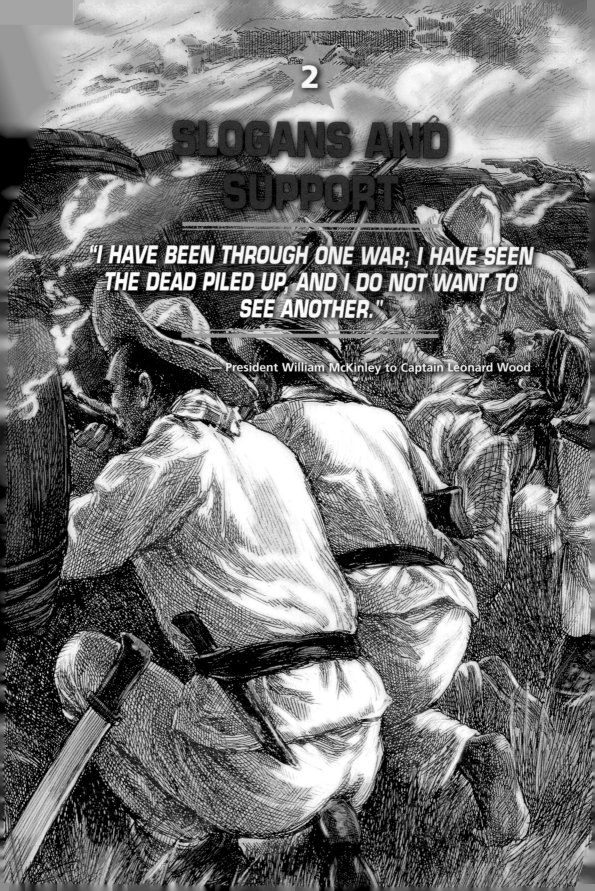

2
SLOGANS AND SUPPORT

"I HAVE BEEN THROUGH ONE WAR; I HAVE SEEN THE DEAD PILED UP, AND I DO NOT WANT TO SEE ANOTHER."

— President William McKinley to Captain Leonard Wood

William Randolph Hearst had built the nation's largest chain of newspapers, most notably the New York Journal. He was looking forward to war with Spain, but it did not immediately follow the *Maine* disaster as he had thought it would. Instead, a long political struggle between those wanting war and those hoping for peace continued for weeks. Much of that struggle played out in the pages of the *New York Journal* and the *New York World*, owned by Hearst's rival Joseph Pulitzer.

William Hearst was famous for his style of yellow journalism, which was designed to capture the emotions of the reader. Hearst also served in the US House of Representatives for New York.

As the newspapers competed for subscribers, sensational stories dominated the headlines. In this kind of journalism, called "yellow journalism," facts were not the focus. It got its name from the fact that the importance of any one story often faded as fast as the cheap paper turned yellow. The *Maine* incident, however, had a powerful and lasting effect on American public opinion. War fever swept across the United States. News of the death count—266 American sailors were killed in the blast—fueled the outrage. Within a few days, the explosion seemed to echo in every part of the angry country. Newspapers owned by William Hearst were, as usual, among the most rabid. Some developed a war slogan that quickly spread across the country: "Remember the *Maine*, to Hell with Spain."[1]

President McKinley, trying to keep the nation calm, named a court of inquiry to investigate the *Maine* disaster. The Spanish government quickly appointed its own committee to probe the matter, hoping to appease the Americans and avert war.

The Spanish investigation was limited. U.S. officials denied requests from Spanish officials to have their divers inspect the wreck. The Spanish investigation, which consisted mainly of rowing around the explosion area, compiled only evidence to support that an internal accident destroyed the USS *Maine*.[2]

The American examiners, after a hasty investigation, disagreed. They felt that the ship was destroyed by an external explosion but could not decide who or what had caused the mysterious blast. The case was puzzling. All witnesses agreed that no other ship or boat had approached the *Maine*. Also, although guards had been on deck, none of the survivors had seen the trail of a torpedo.

The *Leader*, the chief newspaper of Cleveland, Ohio, took the same view as most American papers: "The explosion which destroyed the *Maine* was the result of the cowardly Spanish conspiracy, and the Report of the Court of Inquiry will not tend to destroy that belief."[3]

President McKinley considered the court's conclusions at a closed meeting with his advisors and naval officers. They huddled over the reports for hours. McKinley pondered the results through the weekend. On Monday, he sent the report to Congress, along with a presidential message. The congressmen were astonished. McKinley, in spite of the *Maine* catastrophe, said only what he had been saying for a year. He asked for "deliberate consideration" and took a line of restraint and caution.[4] Congress, along with the newspapers and the American people, joined in a burst of resentment at President McKinley's attitude toward the situation.

In Virginia, a mob of outraged citizens burned effigies of McKinley and his chief advisor, Mark Hanna. In other states, McKinley's portrait was torn from walls and destroyed. Some visitors to the House and Senate galleries in Washington, D.C., came wrapped in American flags to show their respect for the *Maine* disaster.[5]

The destruction of the battleship brought problems between Spain and the United States to a crisis point. Trouble between the nations had existed for a long time. As one newspaper writer wrote, "The Spanish pot has simmered for years. Now at last it has boiled over."[6]

McKinley was the 25th President of the United States. His hope to negotiate with Spain, rather than declare immediate war, was widely criticized.

Foreign Policy

In 1823, the United States had announced a new principle

on foreign policy that became known as the Monroe Doctrine. It proclaimed two main points. First, the Monroe Doctrine claimed that European nations must not try to establish new colonies in the Americas. Second, European powers must not interfere in the affairs of the nations of the Americas. The doctrine, the United States insisted, applied to North and South America and to all islands in the region. In effect, the United States was saying to Europe, "Keep out of our hemisphere."

It had not always been possible for the United States to enforce the Monroe Doctrine. The greatest breach of the doctrine was by France, when the country's troops occupied much of Mexico in 1863. At the time, the United States was much too concerned with its own civil war to engage in a conflict with France. But as soon as the Civil War ended, France prudently pulled its troops out of Mexico.

Many Americans firmly believed in the Monroe Doctrine. Most people felt that Europe should stay out of the "American" part of the globe. Cuba did not really fall within the scope of the Monroe Doctrine. It was not an independent nation and certainly not a new colony. Yet Spanish troops on the island threatened American interests.

In 1854, U.S. President Franklin Pierce approved a public statement called the Ostend Manifesto. It proclaimed that the United States should purchase Cuba from Spain as soon as possible. If Spain

General Juan Rius Rivera was one of the leaders in the second Cuban rebellion.

refused to sell, the United States should simply seize the island. There was wide support for this idea in the American South since several U.S. leaders wanted to annex Cuba as a new slave state. Slavery had been a large part of the work force of the southern states. Adding another slave state would have been a way of enlarging America's commitment to slavery. The implied threat to seize Cuba added to the uproar started in 1854 by the Kansas-Nebraska Act, which made slavery possible in two new U.S. territories. Antislavery forces strongly opposed the Ostend idea, and the Ostend Manifesto added to the growing conflict over slavery between the North and the South. Pierce took no further action to gain Cuba and the approach of the Civil War caused the idea to be lost and forgotten.

Soon after the Civil War, President Ulysses S. Grant listened seriously to suggestions for American intervention to "free Cuba." An invasion of the island might have been an easy way to draw attention away from hard economic times and political scandals in the United States. But nothing came of these proposals. Tyrannical Spanish government and cruel repression drove the Cubans to revolt between 1868 and 1878 in what became known as the Ten Years' War. Revolution broke out again in 1895. The Cuban patriot Jose Marti, who had written reports for the *New York Sun,* was killed in a battle of this revolt, further angering Americans.

Cuba was ruled directly by Spain through the appointment of a series of governors known as "captains-general." They were actually dictators. Cubans were given no real voice in their own government. At times, bands of Spanish soldiers roamed the island burning and looting. Slavery was not completely abolished until 1886. From time to time, the Spanish government promised reforms, but progress existed more on paper than in actual life.

Some people in the United States wanted to replace Spanish control with strong American influence on the island. Other Americans remembered their nation's Revolutionary War against England and sympathized with the

Cubans. Among many American citizens, there was a vague but genuine desire to free Cuba.

In addition, countless Americans were enraged over the cruelty of General Valeriano Weyler, who had been sent from Spain to suppress the Cuban rebels. Weyler's measures were ruthless. He was known for herding much of the island's population into prison camps and committing massacres in many villages. American anger, fanned by gruesome accounts of such incidents in newspapers, finally forced the man now known as "Weyler the Butcher" from Cuba.

Other Americans had different interests. Certain businessmen saw profits to be earned on the island, while a few were angry about money they had lost in Cuba because of the revolt. Sugarcane plantations, some owned by Americans, now stood unused. A few had been burned by revolutionary guerrillas—badly equipped, ill-trained, and often hungry bands of fighters—seeking Cuban independence.

American publishers such as Joseph Pulitzer and William Randolph Hearst viewed the Cuban struggle as an opportunity to sell large numbers of newspapers. They covered their front pages with exaggerated tales of horror from Cuba.

To make the Cuban scene more vivid to American readers, Hearst sent artist Frederic Remington to the island to illustrate Cuban suffering. After some time, Remington wanted to return. He telegraphed this to Hearst, adding that he did not think there would be a war. He received a prompt reply from the publisher telling him to stay where he was and continue drawing. Hearst said, "You furnish the pictures, and I'll furnish the war."[7]

A large group of Americans had dreams of an American empire with lands and outposts in all parts of the world. They looked longingly at Cuba and Puerto Rico in the Caribbean. The idea of an American canal across the Isthmus of Panama in Central America was becoming popular. Cuba would be important for the canal, serving as a naval base, a refueling base, and a supply center for merchant ships. Gazing eastward, some Americans saw Hawaii and the Philippines in the Pacific as stepping-stones to China and Japan. "Manifest Destiny," a term used to describe the relentless American push westward across North America, now seemed to be stretching across the Pacific Ocean to the west and into the Caribbean to the south.

In addition, among those Americans who were proponents of Manifest Destiny, an even more aggressive group existed that simply felt the United States should flex its muscles for the world to see before starting any military conquest. This group came to be called jingoes.

Jingo Voices

A jingo is a person who boasts of his patriotism loudly and excessively, eagerly favoring a nation being prepared for war. Jingoes usually support an aggressive foreign policy and want to dominate other nations.

Throughout history, different countries have had some jingoes urging conquest and talking fiercely about such matters as "national honor" and "defending the flag." The United States was home to an unusually large number of jingoes in the 1890s. The word "jingoism," fairly rare today, became common in newspapers and magazines at that time.

Not all Americans were jingoes. Many did not want war, felt that building an empire was a terrible mistake, and saw no honor in military strength for the sake of itself. Such citizens were called antiexpansionists because they felt that America should be content with its present borders. Today it is more common to speak of "doves" who work for peace, and "hawks" who are working for war.

Part of the jingoism that helped bring about the Spanish-American War sprang from a feeling that life was dull. The men who fought in the American Civil War, despite all the suffering, had shared a great struggle. They were decorated with medals and showered with praise and honor. As memories of war's pain faded, a new generation of Americans longed for their own glorious adventure. They wanted to be heroes themselves—not just the sons or nephews of Civil War veterans.

Influential Positions

By December 1897, Admiral Sicard, commander of the North Atlantic fleet, expected war with Spain was coming soon. Sicard was making all the preparations he could.

Others in the US government were preparing, as well. When war finally came, John Hay was ready. He was the American ambassador in London who was to become secretary of state in 1898. He gained Britain's promise not to get involved if America went to war with Spain. Later, in a letter to Theodore Roosevelt,[8] Hay called the struggle with Spain "a splendid little war."[9] Hay himself had watched the Civil War from the sidelines as a secretary to Abraham Lincoln. But he never had actual experience, splendid or otherwise, in battle.

Theodore Roosevelt also had no experience in war. But he was eagerly looking for an army to lead, and later described the conflict with Spain as "not much of a war, but the only one we have."[10] Roosevelt, serving in his first national position as Assistant Secretary of the Navy, was aggravated at the president's patience in dealing with Spain. "McKinley," he said, "has no more backbone than a chocolate éclair."[11]

An Un-Diplomatic Letter

At the time hostilities were brewing between Spain and the United States, the Spanish minister (ambassador) in Washington was Enrique Dupuy de Lome, an aristocratic professional diplomat. De Lome had done his best to present the Spanish side of the Cuban problem to Americans, especially to President McKinley.

Ambassador de Lome had a difficult job. The Spanish king, Alfonso XIII, was only a boy, so royal power rested with his widowed mother, Queen Regent Maria Cristina. The monarchy had little strength. More powerful was a parliament elected by aristocrats, a cabinet mostly made up of military leaders, and a prime minister who tried to bring the groups to agreement. But the whole government was changeable, uncertain, and controlled by a small ruling class. De Lome followed the official Spanish policy of promising almost anything to quiet American complaints about oppression in Cuba. He knew Spain had no intention of really improving Cuban conditions. Words and empty promises were to be the delay tactic.

The ambassador, however, had strong personal feelings about Cuba. He wrote his opinions in a letter to a friend, a Spanish journalist who was

Assistant Secretary of the Navy Theodore Roosevelt is shown in his office.

visiting Havana. In Cuba, a secretary who was a secret rebel sympathizer opened the letter and then forwarded it to Cuban rebels in the United States. Of the American president, de Lome wrote that McKinley is "weak and a bidder for the admiration of the crowd, besides being a would-be politician who tries to leave a door open behind himself while keeping on good terms with the jingoes of his party."[12] When de Lome learned that his letter was to be published, he resigned before it could appear.

When de Lome's letter was published in American newspapers, the letter was a bombshell. *The New York Journal* printed it on the front-page with the headline, "The Worst Insult to the United States in History."[13] Other newspapers printed and reprinted a ditty about him:

> Dupuy de Lome, Dupuy de Lome,
> what's this I hear of you?
>
> Have you been throwing mud again,
> is what they're saying true?
>
> Get out, I say, get out before I start to fight.
>
> Just pack your few possessions
> and take a boat for home.
>
> I would not like my boot to use but—
> oh—get out, de Lome!?[14]

One leader of the Cuban revolt said, "The de Lome letter is a great thing for us."[15] The rebels were delighted to see Americans freshly outraged by Spanish insolence.

The Spanish government sent a prompt apology to the United States. McKinley himself said nothing about the letter, but the public outcry continued.

Apart from the disrespect for President McKinley, the letter clearly revealed Spain's "words and delays" policy. De Lome felt that negotiation with the Cubans was useless and wanted a Spanish military victory to save the colony for Spain. Americans began to doubt anything promised by the Spaniards.

American Goals for Cuba

The United States had said often that the situation in Cuba was intolerable. But what exactly did Americans want for the island and its inhabitants?

The idea of making Cuba part of the United States was a very old one. Thomas Jefferson, third president of the United States and the chief author of the Declaration of Independence, had written, "I confess that I have ever looked on Cuba as the most interesting addition which could ever be made to our system of states."[16]

The same desire resurfaced again when the Ostend Manifesto was proposed in 1854. This time the message to Spain was blunt: "Sell Cuba or America will take it by force."

Yet the notion of simply seizing Cuba and making it a United States territory seemed to go against American ideals. Only radical jingoes wanted that. Fully supporting the revolt for Cuban independence also had problems. The Cuban rebels had destroyed some property owned by Americans. It was clear that the rebels were violent and brutal. But were they also dangerously anti-American? Were they opposed to American business interests?

One appealing idea was to make Cuba a self-governing state within the Spanish empire. Canada seemed to offer an excellent model. While today Canada is a self-governing nation, Britain ruled Canada completely until 1867, when Canada gained control of its domestic affairs. Britain continued to govern Canada's foreign affairs at that time. As Canada was to Great Britain, so Cuba might be to Spain. This was the most popular solution, and the Spanish government had seemed to react favorably to the idea. Nothing had actually happened as a result, however, aside from riots in Havana by Spaniards who disliked the idea.

Now, the de Lome letter showed that Spain had no intention of creating a Cuba somewhat like Canada. In fact, Spain really did not intend to do anything. Cuban independence seemed the only answer.

In the midst of the national uproar caused by the *Maine* explosion, the de Lome letter, and more violence in Cuba, McKinley had to act even though he still did not think that war was inevitable. He sent a bill to Congress requesting $50 million to be spent for defense. On March 9, 1898, the bill was passed. More than half the new spending was used to increase the size of the Navy with troop transports, colliers, dispatch boats, patrol craft, and more.

The purchasing was entrusted to Theodore Roosevelt, who had become the most energetic assistant secretary of the Navy the nation had ever seen. The obscure Naval Auxiliary Board was now one of the most productive federal offices. He negotiated not only with steamship lines and tug operators, but with members of the New York Yacht Club for five of their steam-powered yachts, the fastest vessels afloat, paying as much as double the original price.

A few days later, the new Spanish ambassador arrived in Washington to replace the disgraced de Lome. Ambassador Polo de Bernabe presented his credentials to McKinley, who read him a little speech of welcome. De Bernabe promptly cabled a message to Madrid, the Spanish capital. "A most gracious address," he said of McKinley's greeting. "I fear, nevertheless, that the acts will not bear out the words."[17]

He was right. Senator Redfield Proctor, a Republican from Vermont, had just returned to Washington after visiting Cuba. He made a full report to the Senate, speaking for several hours in a quiet, toneless voice.

Proctor explained to the US Senate that the condition of Cuba's countryside was "desolation

This photograph captures the plight of the starving Cubans.

and distress, misery and starvation." He also described the horrors of the camps established by General Weyler as "virtual prison yards."[18] He vividly told of the poverty and poor living conditions rampant in Cuba.

An Ultimatum

In late March 1898, President McKinley sent a stern message to Madrid. Responsibility and possible payment for the *Maine* could be settled by arbitration, as Spain had proposed. But the condition of Cuba and its inhabitants would no longer be tolerated by the United States. If Spain did not change its Cuban policies and show results at once, McKinley would "lay the whole matter before Congress."[19] In other words, he would ask for a declaration of war. McKinley set April 15 as the deadline for Spain to make the requested changes in Cuba.

McKinley presented four main demands:
1. Spain must grant an armistice—truce—in

Cuba to last until October. President McKinley would supervise and arbitrate any matters involving this.

2. Spain would end the reconcentration camp policy in Cuba. Spain would also provide massive relief aid to the country.

3. If peace terms between Spain and the rebels were not concluded by October, McKinley would settle the matter.

4. If necessary, McKinley would approach the rebels directly to ask their participation.[20]

The demands did not include the independence of Cuba. But Spain's departure from the island seemed understood in the American message.

By now, events were moving too rapidly, and angrily, for diplomats to stop. On April 20, 1898, after the deadline had passed with no response, both Congress and McKinley demanded that Spain withdraw all troops from Cuba. Before this message could be delivered, Spain told the American ambassador to leave Spain.

Spain announced war against the United States on April 24. The next day, the American Congress declared that war had actually existed since April 21. It was the only retroactive declaration of war in the history of the United States.

Amid all the excitement and war fever, Senator Henry M. Teller proposed an amendment to the war resolution. He wanted the law to forbid any American acquisition of Cuba. His proposal was passed. No one at the time was much concerned with the future of Cuba, but later, this law would prove important.

A little more than two months after the sinking of the *Maine,* America had begun what many of its citizens would look on as the start of a great adventure. The New York *Sun* wrote, "We are all jingos now, and the head jingo is the [Honorable] William McKinley."[21]

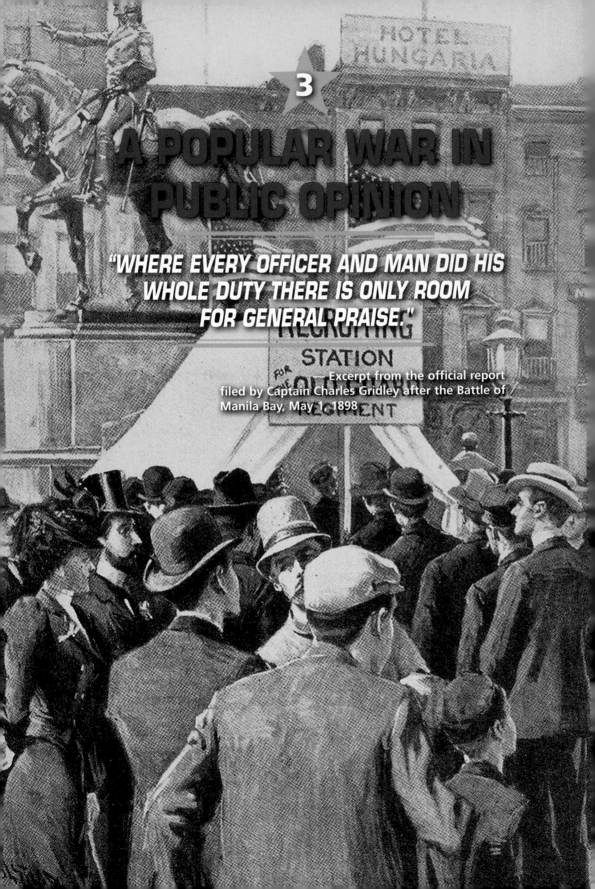

3

A POPULAR WAR IN PUBLIC OPINION

"WHERE EVERY OFFICER AND MAN DID HIS WHOLE DUTY THERE IS ONLY ROOM FOR GENERAL PRAISE."

— Excerpt from the official report filed by Captain Charles Gridley after the Battle of Manila Bay, May 1, 1898

New recruits were desperately needed to supplement the American army, which numbered only 28,000 men. McKinley had called for 125,000 volunteers to supplement the regular army. There were so many willing volunteers, this quota was easily fulfilled. American men went to war in the spring of 1898 as eagerly as if they were going to a party. Parades of young men followed brass bands to army recruiting offices. There had never been so popular a war in America among citizens, banking, and industry.

Before the hostilities actually began, most financial and industrial leaders of America had opposed war, thinking it might be bad for business. Now, they rallied to the flag. In New York's big business district, Wall Street bankers and brokers organized and paid for a special company of volunteers. Mrs. Helen Gould, widow of capitalist Jay Gould and one of America's richest women, donated $100,000 to help the war effort.[1]

There were a few scattered protests against American imperialism. One of the most vocal protesters was Samuel Clemens, popularly known by his pen name Mark Twain. Some opponents of the war, including Clemens and Andrew Carnegie, organized themselves into the American Anti-Imperialist League. They were in the minority, though. Most Americans seemed eager to enter the war.

The society pages of newspapers even carried war-related items. Wealthy readers with summer homes in Newport, Rhode Island, and Bar Harbor, Maine, were warned that the New England coast might be subject to bombardment by the Spanish Navy.[2] Spain had a fleet of warships believed to be anchored in the Azores Islands, in the eastern Atlantic Ocean. The New York paper *World* told readers that Spanish ships could bombard American seaside resort towns. Fears about attacks on New York or Philadelphia, major cities whose harbors were almost undefended, were somewhat more realistic.[3]

No one, including the U.S. Navy, knew much about the Spanish fleet except that it was one of the world's larger naval forces. There were two squadrons, one in the Atlantic and another in the Asian Pacific.

Meanwhile, the U.S. Navy was already blockading Cuba, halting any ships bound to or from the island. No military supplies or soldiers were permitted to pass. American ships were believed to be more modern than those of Spain. The $50 million Congress had given McKinley earlier for military purposes had been spent mostly on the U.S. Navy. Now, the government rushed to spend much more, buying up all kinds of craft that might haul American soldiers to Cuba in the near future. Tampa, Florida, was selected as the gathering place for ships and men who were eventually bound for Cuba.

Paymasters and Quartermasters

Although it had been clear for a long time that war might come, America was quite unprepared. American taxpayers had always hated supporting armed forces in peacetime. Now, the army was embarrassed to find it had fewer than one hundred trained quartermasters to handle the huge task of supplying the expanded forces. Soon, the situation in Tampa turned into a complete tangle as trainloads of food, tents, cots, medical supplies, and arms converged on the town to wait in railroad yards. There was no one to unload the supplies, and no system of keeping track of them.

One of the new pay-masters was particularly worthy of note. In May 1898, Richard R. Wright Sr. was commissioned a major in the U.S. Army and appointed by President McKinley to be paymaster of the United States Volunteers in the United States Army. Wright was the first African American to be named paymaster of the Army.

An Instant Victory

On May 1, 1898, hardly a week after the declaration of war, Americans were startled by newspapers proclaiming a great American naval victory. The astonished and puzzled public read about a battle in a place most had never heard of, led by an officer just as unfamiliar. It all happened roughly 10,000 miles (16,093 km) away from Cuba, which was where the American public had expected the action to take place.

Where were the Philippines and what did they have to do with Cuba? Who was this Commodore George Dewey? How could this victory have happened so fast?

American humorist and journalist F. P. Dunne, whose "Mr. Dooley" newspaper sketches expressed his social and political views, wrote in one column, "I thought Philippines were some kind of canned goods."[4] Americans, quickly brushing up on their geography, learned that the Philippines were a group of seven thousand islands with an area twice the size of Florida. The chief seaport was the large and thriving city of Manila.

The Philippines first became known to Europeans in 1521, when the Spanish explorer Ferdinand Magellan arrived. Malay people inhabited the islands. Centuries before, Chinese ships had visited the islands. There had also been frequent contact with other regions of Southeast Asia. Some of the native people were Hindus. Others were Muslims.

The Spaniards had gone through centuries of war against the Muslim Moors from Morocco, who once occupied much of Spain. To the Spaniards, it seemed that the Muslim inhabitants of these new islands must also be Moors, and that is what they mistakenly called them—Moros, another form of the word. The Spaniards regarded the Philippine "Moors" as traditional enemies.

Spanish conquest of the region began forty years later, and gradually, the islands became Spain's possession. Many of the Filipino people accepted the Catholic religion prevalent in Spain and a smaller number adopted the Spanish language as well.

In 1898, Commodore George Dewey sailed a small fleet of American warships from the British-controlled port of Hong Kong across the South China Sea and surprised the Spaniards at Cavite Harbor near Manila. He sunk the whole enemy squadron without the loss of a single American ship or a single American life.

Hero of the Hour

George Dewey, a career naval officer with a solid but little-known record, was suddenly seen as a new American hero. Congress ordered a commemorative sword presented to him, and he was immediately promoted to the rank of Rear Admiral. Newspapers printed verses dedicated to him. A sculptor even made a bronze bust of the hero and sold thousands of plaster copies.

After drawing his fleet into an attacking position, Dewey had given a command to the captain of his flagship by proclaiming, "You may fire when you are ready, Gridley."[5] Dewey's command soon appeared in books and magazines. Young boys playing naval games in schoolyards often shouted "Fire, Gridley" at each other. America had its first naval hero since Admiral David G. Farragut of the Civil War.

In darkness, Dewey's ships had steamed silently into broad Manila Bay. There, they had waited for light. When dawn broke, the sailors saw the domes and church towers of the city but no Spanish warships. Even this early in the morning, the tropical heat was intense. Since all portholes had been closed on the American ships, the insides seemed as hot as furnaces to the sailors. One man told his fellow soldiers that they need not fear death and the flames of the underworld "for Hell ain't no hotter than this."[6]

Charles Julian, an officer on the *Baltimore,* reported that the flags of the American ships suddenly broke out on the top of every mast in the fleet. His commanding officer, Captain John Dyer, called out, "Men, let's see what we can do under the flag."[7]

The *Baltimore* steamed ahead alongside other American warships, such as the *Raleigh, Petrel, Concord,* and *Boston.* Commodore Dewey appeared on the flying bridge—the high platform atop the pilothouse—dressed in a white tropical uniform and a golf cap. He had packed so fast in Hong Kong that his cabin was a jumble of clothes. Somewhere in the heap was his uniform hat.

A puff of smoke suddenly appeared in Manila, and then a shell from a shore battery exploded overhead with an ear-splitting blast. Two other batteries on shore then began firing, but Dewey ignored them. His aim was to destroy Spanish ships. He would not be distracted by other guns.

Dewey's ships swung around a hook of land called Sangley Point. There, he saw the Spanish ships drawn up in a crescent-shaped line. At that moment, a shell, fired from 6 miles (9.6 km) away, curved through the sky and struck the water beyond the fleet. Dewey did not return this fire, but moved on toward the Spanish ships. He knew he had to make every shot count. The nearest supply base for the U.S. Navy was thousands of miles away in San Francisco, California.

Slowly, the American ships moved into place. They maneuvered past dangers such as shallow water and shoals, or hidden sandbars. At last, Commodore Dewey uttered his famous order to Captain Gridley, and the guns began roaring.

Several hours later, the American ships withdrew to safer anchorage, having won a complete victory. Dewey sank or destroyed all seven of the Spanish warships. The Spanish had 167 dead and 214 wounded. Damages to American ships were slight, and only seven American soldiers were wounded. Spain's eastern fleet no longer existed.

George Dewey is the only person in history to be named Admiral of the Navy, which he was named in honor of his victory in Manila Bay.

Taking Chances

This was not only a great victory but also an unlikely one. When Dewey's ships sailed from Hong Kong, a British naval officer there thought the Americans were brave but doomed. At Manila, the odds against the Americans seemed fatal. What chance could Dewey's small squadron have against

Spanish forts that had been guarding the harbor for two hundred years, a fleet of enemy warships, and the dangerous minefields said to make Manila Harbor impassable?

Two years later, Admiral Dewey pointed out that his fleet could easily have been trapped and destroyed by guns from shore batteries in Manila Bay. Their advantage was that the Spaniards had been caught off guard, unready for action.

Dewey, a sailor of great experience, also made an educated guess that later proved important. It was generally believed that entrances to the harbor had been heavily mined with explosives. Ships entering without knowledge of safe routes would be destroyed. Dewey doubted this. He felt the swift currents in the bay would make it almost impossible to plant mines successfully.

Fortunately for the Americans, Dewey was right. There were no minefields in Manila Bay.

Friends in the Right Places

A year before the Battle of Manila Bay was fought, three men connected with military affairs in Washington, DC, had become golfing companions. They were Theodore Roosevelt, Leonard Wood, and George Dewey.

Roosevelt had served as the first U.S. Civil Service commissioner under President Benjamin Harrison, then gained fame as a young police commissioner in New York City. He was now assistant secretary of the U.S. Navy. He was also

The Americans were unexpected at Manila Bay, which helped them win the battle.

widely known as a big-game hunter, amateur cowboy, and author of outdoor adventure books. He even wrote a much-praised naval history of the War of 1812.

Captain Leonard Wood of the army had been appointed assistant attending surgeon to President McKinley, too quiet a job for a man of action. Young Captain Wood had been a fighter against the Apaches in the West and the famed Apache chief Geronimo. Tall, strong, and athletic, Leonard Wood was "a doctor by profession and a soldier by choice."[8]

The third friend was a contrast to the other two. Commodore George Dewey, sixty years old, stood just over 5 feet 2 inches (1.6 m), barely tall enough to meet the navy height requirement. Although anything but heroic looking, Commodore Dewey was very concerned about his appearance. It was said he was the best-dressed officer in the navy, and the "creases of his trousers were as sharp as his views on naval warfare."[9]

Apart from their interest in warfare, the three men had something in common. All three craved fame and glory. Roosevelt and Wood longed to lead a heroic army to war. Dewey, bored with more than thirty years of dull service in the peacetime navy, wanted to command warships in mighty naval battles.

At the time, the three men had little opportunity for greatness. President McKinley was trying his best to avoid war. So Roosevelt and Wood bided their time and worked actively in jingoist politics. Roosevelt also did all he could to secure an important command for his friend Commodore Dewey. Through Roosevelt's efforts, Dewey was at last given command of the Pacific Squadron. Dewey went with a fleet to the Pacific and waited impatiently.

Roosevelt's behind-the-scenes role in the Battle of Manila Bay took place on February 25, 1898. War was brewing but two months away. Secretary of the Navy John D. Long, the official that Roosevelt assisted, had a medical appointment. He left his office, telling Roosevelt to take charge for the rest of the day. Impulsive Roosevelt did not waste this opportunity. He quickly sent his friend Commodore Dewey a cablegram relaying an official Navy order:

> Dewey, Hongkong:
>
> Secret and confidential. Order the squadron ... to Hongkong. Keep full of coal. In the event of declaration of war [on] Spain, your duty will be to see that the Spanish squadron does not leave the Asiatic coast, and then offensive operations in Philippine Islands ...
>
> ROOSEVELT[10]

During the three or four hours that Roosevelt was in charge of the U.S. Navy, he sent out one message after another to distant commanders. He ordered fuel, extra ammunition, guns, and the recruitment of seamen. He almost put the entire navy on a state of alert as it had not known since the Civil War.

The next day, when Secretary Long returned, he discovered that Roosevelt had "come very near causing more of an explosion than happened to the *Maine*."[11] Long seemed annoyed, but he did not reprimand or discharge Roosevelt. It was already too difficult for Long to halt Roosevelt's orders. Instead, he decided never to leave Roosevelt in sole charge of the navy again.

Only two months later, the nation would be amazed by the speed with which Commodore Dewey attacked the Spanish ships in Manila Bay. Almost no one knew of Roosevelt's unauthorized part in the victory until long afterward.

Roosevelt resigned his navy position. With his friend Leonard Wood, he now began organizing the fighting group that would become the war's most famous soldiers—the Rough Riders.

A Need for Supply Bases

The U.S. Navy learned much from Dewey's early victory. First, it was clear how lucky the United States had been.

According to the international laws that most nations agreed on, American warships could not have remained in any neutral port once war with Spain was declared. The British would have closed Hong Kong to them, and the Japanese would have forbidden Yokohama. Perhaps American vessels could have forced their way into Chinese harbors, because China seemed too weak to stop them. But this was a poor solution at best and could have had serious international consequences.

Clearly, the U.S. Navy could not operate for long in the Asian Pacific without supply bases closer than California. If Dewey had not won a quick victory, he would simply have run out of ammunition and the coal needed to fuel the steam engines of his ships.

As war drew nearer, the possibility had alarmed Dewey. The USS *Baltimore* was the ship carrying most of the squadron's ammunition. It was delayed on its path to meet Dewey in Hong Kong. On April 22, Dewey was informed that war might break out at any moment, and still the *Baltimore* had not arrived.

That same afternoon the ship sailed into view. The anchor had hardly dropped before Dewey had boats alongside it and men aboard to unload the precious supplies. Even while the unloading was taking place, the ship was being painted wartime gray—colorless and difficult to see on the horizon—to ready it for battle.

When the Spanish-American War was over, Americans would remember the close call at Manila Bay. Naval bases in distant parts of the Pacific would be important war prizes the United States would seek. The Philippine Islands would be one such foothold, but other islands would be needed as well.

Seizing Sangley Point

Only a few years before the Battle of Manila Bay, a native movement for independence, similar to Cuba's, had started in the islands. After several bloody battles, the rebels were suppressed by Spain, but a revolution for independence was still smoldering when Dewey sailed past the city of Manila. Americans knew almost nothing about the determination of the Filipino people to have their own, independent country. But they would learn a lot more in the coming years.

Before Dewey's squadron sailed from Manila Bay, he seized a small point of land to use as a base for future operations. This little strip, a peninsula called Sangley Point near the city of Cavite, was a major step in America's new road to a larger empire.

4

CAVALRY VOLUNTEERS AND VETERANS

"ROUGH! TOUGH! WE'RE THE STUFF! WE'RE THE SCRAPPERS; NEVER GET ENGOUH! W-H-O-O-E-E!"

—Rough Rider cheer

As soon as war seemed inevitable, Theodore Roosevelt made the surprise move of resigning his position as assistant secretary of the Navy. He arranged to enlist for a brand-new regiment: the 1st Volunteer Cavalry. It had been a special dream of Roosevelt for years that one day he would lead his own regiment in the army. In his imagination, this mounted regiment would be made up of tough outdoor heroes, including cowboys, trail scouts, and mountain men. Of course, he would be their commander. Now the war with Spain gave him a chance to live his dream and make it a reality.

Although Roosevelt had no experience at all as an army officer, he arranged to have himself commissioned as a lieutenant colonel. He was second in command to his friend Colonel Leonard Wood, who would actually lead the new regiment.

The official name of this force was the First United States Volunteer Cavalry, but newspaper writers quickly gave it more than a dozen nicknames. "Teddy's Terrors" was one, and "Teddy's Texas Tarantulas" was another. Roosevelt let it be known that he disliked the nickname "Teddy," so the new force became "Roosevelt's Rough Riders," and finally just "Rough Riders."

The nickname Teddy, whether Roosevelt liked it or not, also stuck. The Rough Riders themselves greeted and cheered their lieutenant colonel as Teddy. So did well-wishers across the country. Newspaper journalists began using Teddy, and the nickname became permanent.

The *New York Press,* a newspaper politically opposed to Roosevelt, nicknamed the new lieutenant colonel Teethadore because of the rows of white teeth Roosevelt displayed when he grinned, which was often. The editor pointed out that Colonel Wood "is lost sight of entirely" beside the glitter of Roosevelt.[1] Wood did not mind. He went to San Antonio, Texas, to organize a "muster camp," a reception and training post for the volunteers.

Roosevelt promptly resigned from the Navy Department and ordered a splendid uniform from a fashionable New York tailor. He chose which applications to accept from the huge number of enlistments pouring in from all parts of the country. For every Rough Rider accepted, twenty other hopefuls were refused.

Although Roosevelt was certainly choosing cowboys and buffalo hunters, he also wanted his regiment to have a social "tone." He reserved fifty places for "gentlemen" from Harvard and other Ivy League schools, plus members of exclusive New York clubs.[2] He happily accepted a national tennis champion, an Ivy League football quarterback, and the former captain of the Columbia University rowing team.[3]

Having quickly filled the regimental ranks with one thousand eager volunteers, Roosevelt set out for San Antonio. On arrival, he saw a sign in the railway station, This Way to Camp of Roosevelt's Rough Riders.

Some of the new Rough Riders were disappointed when they saw Roosevelt for the first time. "He wore glasses," one onlooker sneered, regarding glasses as a silly Eastern notion.[4] They soon learned, however, that he could ride rough with the toughest men.

Roosevelt was talented in gaining personal publicity, but sometimes stories would get twisted. It is no wonder that a newspaper in Madrid, the capital of Spain, became confused. "The Commander-in-Chief of the American Army is one Ted Roosevelt, a New York policeman ... He was born in Holland, near Haarlem," the newspaper told Spanish readers, mistaking that city for Harlem, New York. The article continued: "Now he goes about the country with a bodyguard of toughs, known as 'rough rioters.'"[5]

Almost three fourths of the Rough Riders were actually cowboys. Like their lieutenant colonel, they had some stubborn habits. They insisted on carrying their own weapons instead of army guns. Also, most of them scorned army hats and wore their own big sombreros.

Life in the Rough Rider camp began before dawn. There were many hours of cavalry drill daily and considerable time dedicated to bronco busting. In the evening Roosevelt and other officers gave educational lectures if anyone wanted to listen.

The Rough Riders seemed to embody the American spirit and the romance of the Wild West. The Rough Riders were commonly portrayed in Buffalo Bill's Wild West Show.

Meanwhile, things were getting rough in San Antonio. Two Texas troopers of the Rough Riders shot a mirrored saloon "to smithereens" and others shot out all the lights at an outdoor concert. Colonel Leonard Wood said, "If we don't get them quickly to Cuba to fight Spaniards, they'll be fighting one another."[6]

Then, exciting news came from Washington, arousing war whoops and a volley of revolver shots in the camp. The Rough Riders were ordered to proceed to Tampa, Florida, to board ships. As to where these ships would be sailing, the orders said, "Destination unknown."[7] The men hoped it was Cuba.

Not an Easy Ride

The Rough Riders were supposed to be ready to leave San Antonio at five A.M. on May 29, 1898. Seven different trains awaited them. No one had imagined how difficult it would be to persuade twelve hundred horses and mules to board the right train car. The last mule was put aboard its train at midnight.

The trains had no passenger cars, so the men would have to follow later. A thousand men and officers lay down beside the tracks to catch what sleep they could. At six A.M. on May 30, twenty-four hours after they first arrived, trains carrying the men chugged out of the station.

They continued their sluggish journey for four full days through sweltering weather across the South. Theodore Roosevelt sent gallon after gallon of coffee through the cars. At the many stations where the trains paused, hordes of people passed free watermelons and other gifts through the train windows.

Crowds lined the tracks to get a glimpse of Roosevelt and the Rough Riders. Many in the crowd were elderly Civil War veterans in old Confederate uniforms, waving American flags. Roosevelt commented, "Only thirty-three years ago these men had been enemies of the Union. It took a war to heal the scars."[8] Many others would comment that this new war was a way of getting over the last one. It was a step toward reuniting the nation.

Finally, on the evening of June 2, the caravan of trains came to a halt 6 miles (9.6 km) from Tampa. The last leg of the journey was completed on horseback with equipment piled into every farm wagon that could be found.

If the Rough Riders had expected a welcome in Tampa, they were disappointed. No one had prepared for them. Roosevelt and Wood searched acres of tents before finding the regiment's assigned space. The weary riders pitched their camp in total darkness.

The men awoke in the morning to a surprise. Around them, for miles in every direction, stretched a city of tents. This was the largest assembly of U.S. troops since the Civil War. Twenty-five thousand soldiers were gathered on the flat, sandy plain outside Tampa. There were a few scrubby pine trees, mostly hung with moss, but no other shade.

This photo shows the Rough Riders traveling to Tampa. They were packed into open railway cars.

Some men were reminded of *Arabian Nights*, a book of fantastic tales set in Arabia, in the Middle East. They stood ankle deep in sand that resembled a desert. In the distance they saw domes and minarets—Muslim towers—shimmering like a mirage in the hazy air.

It was not a mirage. The Moorish-looking vision was the Tampa Bay Hotel, a five-hundred-room tourist attraction on the edge of the city. It had five ballrooms and a peacock park.

In the hotel lived Brigadier General William Rufus Shafter, commander of the huge Fifth Army corps. He suffered from many ailments and weighed over 300 pounds (136 kg), but President McKinley had chosen him to lead the army through the hills of Cuba. Shafter was in command at Tampa because of the army's seniority policy: Important posts were automatically given to the oldest generals.

In Tampa, Theodore Roosevelt saw empty ships at anchor in the harbor with no supplies loaded. He found that the nearest railroad tracks ended 9 miles (14.5 km) away from the docks. He wrote in his diary, "No words can paint the confusion. ... A breakdown of both the military and railroad system of the country."[9]

The Rough Riders made the best of the situation. They put on a show of fancy cavalry tactics for the other men waiting in Tampa. The line of horsemen that performed stretched 2 miles (3.2 km) long.

Bottleneck at Tampa Bay

Disturbing news suddenly came to Roosevelt and Colonel Wood. General Shafter had decided to send no horses to Cuba, except a few for high-ranking officers. Also, there would be room on the ships for only 560 of the 1,000 Rough Riders.

Some soldiers' dreams of glory in battle were shattered. "We would rather crawl on all fours than not go," said one Rough Rider.[10] Roosevelt and Wood had to choose five hundred men who would wait in Tampa until other arrangements could be made. Some of the toughest men were so upset at being left behind that they simply sat down and cried.

General Shafter had been delaying the departure of the troops. McKinley finally lost patience and sent an order for him to depart at once. The general replied that the army would embark as soon as the ships could get up steam. All the ships were powered by steam produced by burning coal. Getting cold engines re-fired was a slow process.

The Rough Riders packed in haste and, by midnight on June 8, 1898, they were assembled with their equipment at the railroad track they had been assigned. No train came. They were sent to another track, waited again, and still saw no train. Finally, just after dawn, some coal cars came, filthy with black dust. The Rough Riders seized them. The cars faced the wrong direction, and there was no place to turn around. The engineers were finally persuaded to back the cars 9 miles (14.5 km) to the port in reverse gear. The soldiers were covered with coal dust from head to foot.

When it turned out that no ship had been provided for the regiment, Colonel Wood jumped into a small launch that was passing. He found a ship, the *Yucatán,* just steaming into port to pick up two other regiments. Wood seized the ship, and marched his men aboard before the other regiments arrived.

Theodore Roosevelt also found two photographers with a huge tripod and camera on the dock. They wanted to get to Cuba to photograph the war in moving pictures, which would be a first. Roosevelt, always alert to publicity, got them aboard.

Troubles and mix-ups affected every transport ship. No one had counted the number of sleeping bunks needed for the men, so sleeping space had to be assigned on the crowded decks. Rations of canned beef were so spoiled that men threw them overboard, adding to garbage that now blocked the harbor canal. The floating beef also attracted sharks and made it impossible for the troops to cool off by swimming.[11] "Most of the [transports] have bands, so we get lots of music," naval cadet Joseph Taussig wrote in his journal, glad to get letters from home. "The troops appear to be comfortable and in good spirits. They cheer upon the least provocation."[12]

When it seemed that nothing else could go wrong, a message arrived cancelling the departure of the troop ships. Two strange warships had been sighted somewhere off Cuba. Could they be Spanish destroyers waiting to ambush the American convoy? No one knew. Late in the hot afternoon of June 14, eight days after the Rough Riders had broken camp to sail, the ships were finally cleared to depart.

They were at last on the way to Cuba. At least most of the troops thought so. Others felt they were headed for Puerto Rico. No one—not even Theodore Roosevelt—was quite sure. Their destination was still secret.

An Odd, But American Armada

Roosevelt wrote in his diary that as he stood on the deck of the *Yucatán,* he felt he would soon help "score the first great triumph of a mighty world-movement."[13] Like other jingoes, Roosevelt had dreams that reached beyond this war. He imagined a powerful America ruling lands far across the globe.

Most of the Rough Riders were much too tired to worry about building empires. Others were too seasick, even though the ocean was calm. Many of the men were jammed below decks with the horses and mules. The mules were for hauling baggage and equipment. Fortunately, only officers took horses along. If Roosevelt had had his way, every Rough Rider would have had a horse. It would have taken another ship to transport them.

When night came, the ships' bands played "The Star-Spangled Banner," and every vessel turned on all its lights. It was a bright parade across the Gulf of Mexico, twenty-six ships strung out in a line almost 30 miles (48 km) long. They ranged from modern cruisers to antique Civil War side-wheelers. General Shafter let them proceed at their own speed, making no effort to keep them in formation. The bright lights at night showed their position to anyone who was looking. Officers of the U.S. Navy, unable to do anything about Shafter's lax orders, feared that a Spanish warship might suddenly appear and sink the whole fleet. The navy warships, escorting the transport ships, announced their worries by semaphore signal flags and through megaphones. General Shafter paid no attention to the navy's complaints.

One writer later said, "Shafter spread over an enormous area himself, and was content to let his

The US Armada gathers in Cuban waters, as they prepare to land.

fleet do the same."[14] Luckily, there were no Spanish warships loose in the Gulf. The American ships sailed on for six days and nights—noisily, brightly, and, thankfully, safely.

On the morning of June 20, the fleet turned sharply southeast. The troops had been comparing their course with maps. They were now sure that their destination was Cuba, possibly Santiago de Cuba far to the east or maybe even Havana.

That day there was trouble on board USS *Iowa* with their steam engine. A manhole gasket blew out, blowing boiling water from the boiler into the engine room. The steam engine still needed to have coal fed into the firebox, though, or the *Iowa* would stop moving. It would have been vulnerable without the valiant work of Fireman Robert Penn. Penn stood on a board thrown across a coal bucket, just 1 foot (30 cm) above the boiling water, risking his life to continue hauling coal into the firebox. He was one of six African Americans awarded the Medal of Honor during the war.

Cheers rang out from the ships as the Cuban coast came into view—steep mountains, blue in the distance, rising sharply more than 1 mile (1.6

km) high on the horizon. Some of the soldiers knew that Cuba was called the Pearl of the Antilles and was considered the most beautiful island close to the American continent.

One of the most famous of the reporters with the fleet, Richard Harding Davis of the *New York Herald,* described what the astonished American soldiers saw from the decks that day:

> Every feature of the landscape was painted in high lights; there was no shading, it was all brilliant, gorgeous, and glaring. The sea was an indigo blue, like the blue in a washtub; the green of the mountains was the green of corroded copper; the scarlet trees were the red of a Tommy's [a British soldier's] jacket, and the sun was like a lime-light in its fierceness.[15]

The soldiers had plenty of time to study this strange land lying just a few miles away. The fleet halted while General Shafter and a few officers went ashore to meet with the leader of the Cuban rebels. They would now plan the American landing and the bombardment of the coast, which would start the next morning.

When evening came, the bands on the decks again played "The Star-Spangled Banner." Then, the musicians burst into the popular song "There'll Be a Hot Time in the Old Town Tonight."[16] The Americans would start creating their own hot time in Cuba at dawn.

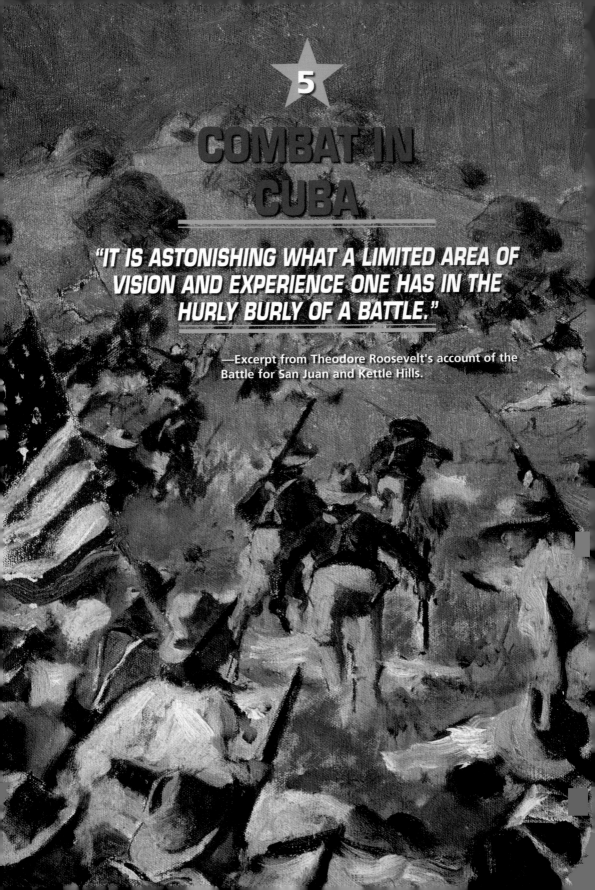

5

COMBAT IN CUBA

"IT IS ASTONISHING WHAT A LIMITED AREA OF VISION AND EXPERIENCE ONE HAS IN THE HURLY BURLY OF A BATTLE."

—Excerpt from Theodore Roosevelt's account of the Battle for San Juan and Kettle Hills.

Soon after dawn, the Naval blockade began shelling the Cuban coast. Their targets were the small villages of Daiquirí and Siboney, a few miles farther east. The bombardment was meant to confuse the Spaniards. They hoped it would mislead them about where the troops were coming ashore. The real target was Daiquirí.

By the first light, the American soldiers saw that Daiquirí was a poor village of shanties with a rickety dock. A small ironworks factory stood near the shore.

Suddenly a tall, thin column of smoke arose from it as the factory's walls crumpled. Spanish soldiers, retreating from the town, had decided to blow up the only building of value.

The American landing was an example of total confusion and mismanagement. Large ships could not approach the beach and there were few small boats. The water was so rough that one soldier later said, "Getting ashore was like jumping off a moving elevator and hoping to land on a floor."[1]

General Shafter made no plans for unloading the horses and mules. They were simply put into the sea with the belief that they would find their own way ashore. Some animals did, but others, confused, swam farther into the ocean.[2] A quick-witted bugler blew a cavalry charge command, and the well-trained horses turned and swam toward the familiar sound. Experienced cavalrymen knew they could ride their horses through the waves. They and their mounts easily reached the beach. Many of the other animals did not. One of Roosevelt's two horses was drowned in the landing and the other hardly survived. He described the landing as "animal torture."[3]

As with so many near disasters in this war, the Americans were often saved from destruction because the Spaniards were equally disorganized. They had left no Spanish rear guard or sharpshooters on the shore. If even a handful of enemy soldiers had defended the beach with rifles, the Americans would have been easy targets as they struggled ashore.

At last, about three thousand soaking-wet American soldiers made it to land and formed up ranks. The army occupied the ruined village. Later in the day, more men from the ships swam, floundered, and waded onto Cuban soil. By sunset, there were about six thousand soldiers trying to sleep on the beach. Their worst enemies that night were biting red ants and land crabs.

The *Yucatán* had sailed away early in the morning, taking much of the personal and regimental baggage of the Rough Riders. Other army groups had similar experiences. Roosevelt himself was left with only the uniform he stood in and a yellow raincoat. Luckily, some essential items—such as his glasses—were sewn inside his hat. For his men's rations, Roosevelt was reduced to approaching Sergeant Mingo Sanders in the 25th Infantry, and requesting that B company share its hard tack.

Among the first things American soldiers discovered on the island were coconuts. An Ohio regiment had been confined on shipboard for two weeks, a very lengthy time for the short voyage from Tampa. They had lived mostly on canned tomatoes. Now, they fell on the coconuts as if they were devouring a feast.

Another discovery was the downpour of tropical rain in Cuba. The Ohioans nicknamed their first stopping place Camp Mud.

The initial major military objective was Santiago de Cuba, Cuba's second-largest city. Much of the Spanish Army was in that region. It was believed that if Santiago de Cuba fell to the Americans, the rest of Cuba would collapse quickly. Reaching it involved a fairly difficult march through jungle in mountainous country.

The first morning, the army was to follow a road about 7 miles (11 km) long. It looked easy on a map. In reality, it led into steep slopes where the tropical sun beat down on the men. Soon the soldiers were abandoning clothes and equipment, dropping mess kits, shirts, and extra ammunition beside the jungle trail. Quickly left behind were the woollen clothes issued by the army to troops bound for the tropics.

Cubans from nearby villages emerged from hiding in the foliage to gather up abandoned property. Revolution and oppressive military government on the island had left the villagers impoverished. They were delighted by the unexpected prizes the soldiers left behind.

The Americans now began meeting Cuban rebel soldiers who emerged from jungle paths to join in the upcoming battles. The Cuban soldiers were poorly dressed in torn trousers, and many were barefoot. They carried machetes—large heavy knives—and woven straw bags. Most of these soldiers were poorly armed.[4] The hungry, outnumbered jungle fighters had held out against the Spanish Army for years. They kept the hope of independence alive on their island.

Battle Begins at Las Guasimas

The first fight of the war, hardly big enough to be called a battle, took place the morning of June 24, 1898, at a deserted village called Las Guasimas. The Spanish had entrenched themselves on a ridge near a mountain pass. The roads the Americans followed led past this position. There were also Spanish snipers, well-trained sharp-shooters, hidden in the jungle on the opposite side of the road from the trenches. Their plan was to catch the Americans in their crossfire.

The Americans advanced in two groups. A regiment of regular army men moved along one road. At the same time, the Rough Riders took an overgrown trail and moved like fighters in the Old West, crouching and dodging from one clump of trees to another. The jungle was sweltering, and the men were curious about strange birdcalls they heard in the thickets.

The Spanish began shooting from their hiding places. Despite dense foliage, they seemed to know where the Americans were. Soon the soldiers realized that the "birds" in the jungle were actually Spanish scouts signaling American positions. At last, the Americans were able to charge the trenches on the ridge. Rifles cracked, and heavier weapons known as Hotchkiss Mountain Guns roared and bellowed. Some soldiers were unnerved by the strange whistle of Spanish bullets. The buzzing noise came from high-speed Mauser bullets, standard for Spanish sharpshooters but unknown to Americans. Also, the Spaniards used smokeless gunpowder, so their shots left no telltale little puffs behind. This, too, was new to Americans.

Once the Americans were free of the forest and able to charge across open ground, the tide of battle shifted abruptly. About fifteen hundred Spaniards suddenly broke from their entrenchments and scattered into the jungle. They were fleeing in the direction of the city of Santiago de Cuba to form new defensive lines.

The general commanding the American regulars, "Fighting Joe" Wheeler, had been a youthful Confederate officer in the Civil War. Now, he seemed to think he was back in that war again, for he shouted, "We've got the damn Yankees on the run!"[5]

The fighting had lasted only two hours, although most of the men thought it took half a day. Sixteen Americans were dead, fifty-two wounded. Soon the newspapers in the United States would be proclaiming a great victory.

Battling on San Juan Heights

The Americans advanced slowly toward the city of Santiago de Cuba. To capture this city, it was necessary first to cross and then to hold a long ridge known as San Juan Heights. Spanish blockhouses and trenches fortified the hill. General Shafter drew a rough sketch of the road and the defenses. He somehow forgot to include another steep ridge, Kettle Hill, which also had a blockhouse and entrenchments. Kettle Hill would soon become important.

The Americans believed that the Spaniards had 12,000 men defending Santiago de Cuba. Cuban rebels, who were helping the Americans by scouting the enemy, said 8,000 more soldiers were on their way from other parts of Cuba to help the Spaniards defend the city. The total American force available for the coming battle numbered 16,000. If the Americans delayed, they would soon be outnumbered.

The American officers met to plan the attack and listen to General Shafter's plans. Just as the meeting was ending, word came that two American generals were stricken with fever. They would have to be replaced. In the shuffling of command that followed this news, Wood became a general and Roosevelt was promoted to full colonel. He wrote, "To my intense delight, I got my regiment!"[6]

Everything now seemed ready for a major victory. But General Shafter and other officers had not considered how difficult it would be to march 16,000 men along a muddy jungle road only 10 feet (3 m) wide. The American advance started before dawn and continued until late at night, men slogging in deep mud.

Finally, they made camp on the brow of a hill with a distant view of San Juan Heights. The next morning would be what Roosevelt called "the great day of my life."[7] Roosevelt was now in full command of the Rough Riders, while Wood led Regular Army troops.

Bugle blasts shattered the calm of dawn. Heavy guns were dragged to the hilltop and prepared for firing. At 6:30, big guns roared, sending flocks of jungle birds into the air with shrill cries. Suddenly General Wood's brigade found itself under a heavy artillery barrage. Shells shrieked and burst, white plumes of smoke shot upward from the Rough Rider ranks, and four men fell to the ground. It would have been suicidal to stay on the hilltop, for the Spanish gunners were deadly accurate. The Americans rushed down the slope to the cover of the jungle.

"The brush was so dense as to be almost impenetrable, and break up all formation," wrote Major Charles Morton of the 4th US Cavalry in his report.[8] From glimpses through the dense trees, it was easy for the Cavalry regiments to mistake the blockhouse on nearby Kettle Hill for Fort San Juan.

Volunteers and army regulars struggled through mud. They saw Cuban rebels who had joined them falling to Spanish fire. As the Americans waded across a stream, a huge hot-air balloon they had launched for spying on the enemy was pierced by shots and crashed down. It smothered some men wading the creek and entangled others in bullet-riddled folds.

Roosevelt's orders were to charge directly up the San Juan Heights. But he found himself at the foot of another hill, the one General Shafter had omitted from his map. The crest of this rise, Kettle Hill, was spouting flame due to the fast repetition of hundreds of Spanish rifles and heavier guns firing. Kettle Hill looked like a small volcano about to erupt, fire spitting down on the Americans.

Most American troops seemed trapped in a hailstorm of bullets, while others were stalled and wavering in their frontal assault on San Juan Heights. To remain caught between two fortified hills was impossible. The Rough Riders had no orders, but their colonel, who had held that rank for just one day, immediately acted on his own.

The Rough Riders charge up Kettle Hill during the Battle at San Juan Heights.

Roosevelt rallied his regiment and charged up the unmapped slope. Bullets whizzed past them as they struggled through barbed wire entanglements. One remark in Roosevelt's recollections of the struggle is especially notable. As he led his regiment's charge up Kettle Hill, he saw that theentanglements of barbed wire, part of the Spanish defense, were being cut by African-American soldiers. In the face of enemy fire, these men were bravely clearing the way.[9] These Black Troopers were at least as far up the slope as the Rough Riders. Then they were together at the top of the hill, engaging with the enemy in fierce hand-to-hand fighting.

As a few remaining Spaniards fled down the slope, the Americans noticed something strange near the crest they had just reached: a huge iron pot probably used in sugar refining. This was how the spot eventually earned the name Kettle Hill.

From this crest there was a full view of San Juan Heights. Clearly, the American assault there was flagging. Some of the men who had just taken Kettle Hill began a deadly assault on the San Juan blockhouse, while others raced toward the main struggle. Rough Riders and Regulars ran down the far slope of Kettle Hill, then charged up the steep San Juan Heights. With them were African-American companies fresh from their assault on Spanish barricades.

At the same time, American troops—mostly Regular Army including the 25th Infantry—were breaking through Spanish lines at a river bend near a village called El Caney. Only 520 Spanish soldiers held El Caney. They faced 4,500 attacking Americans. Still, the defenders stubbornly held their position for eleven hours. When an American assault spearheaded by General A. R. Chaffee's brigade finally swept over the field, Corporal Thomas Butler of the 24th Infantry was credited by eyewitnesses with capturing the Spanish flag at the blockhouse. Only about one hundred Spaniards survived to retreat to Santiago de Cuba. About 320 Spanish soldiers were killed or seriously wounded. Their defending officer, General Vara del Rey, was among the dead.

The Americans at El Caney then joined with the forces attacking San Juan in a frontal assault. In another hour, the battle was over. American troops stood on the San Juan Heights overlooking the city of Santiago de Cuba. It was another victory, but this time at a heavier price: at least 800 American casualties, perhaps more than 1,000. Also, some of the Cuban rebels who joined the American attack had fallen. Meanwhile, several trenches were filled with Spanish casualties who had bravely defended the Heights.

The victory went down in American history as the Battle of San Juan Hill. The Rough Riders have received more than their fair share of credit for the victory, because their commander was such a genius at getting publicity. "What most people do not know is that the brunt of the fighting was borne by the soldiers of the 9th and 10th Cavalry Regiments," wrote commentator Paul Matthews in 2014. "One eyewitness has written: 'If it had not been for the Negro Cavalry, the Rough Riders would have been exterminated. The 10th Cavalry fought for 48 hours under fire from Spaniards who were in brick forts on the hill'."[10]

Black Troopers in Battle

The important work of African-American volunteers during the Spanish-American War has yet to be recognized widely. Their role in the armed forces was not yet as part of an army with integrated races. It would be almost fifty years more and two wars later that black and white soldiers would serve together within one integrated army unit. During the Spanish-American War, apart from a few African Americans in the Navy, the only "Black Troopers" (as they were called) were in two cavalry regiments and two infantry regiments that had been set up since the American Civil War.

The Black Troopers of the 9th and 10th Cavalry and the 24th and 25th Infantry regiments were a small percentage of the over 250,000 soldiers and 11,000 officers who served in the Spanish-American War. But they made major contributions on both land and sea. Some of them were among the army's more experienced soldiers, having served in action in units against the Apache, Comanche, and other tribes in the American West.

By the 1890s some of their officers were men of color, like the 9th Cavalry chaplain. Born the son of slaves, George Prioleau became a teacher, pastor, and later a professor of theology at Wilberforce University in Ohio. President Grover

Cleveland appointed him chaplain of the 9th Cavalry in 1895. Captain Prioleau was with the 9th when they mustered in Georgia and Florida for deployment in the Spanish-American War. Stricken with malaria, Prioleau was unable to go to Cuba. Upon recovering, he served as a recruitment officer. Through editorials and letters to newspapers, Captain Prioleau publicly challenged the hypocrisy of fighting for Cuba's liberation while the USA maintained racial segregation against black soldiers. "When the 9th returned from the Spanish-American war, they were cheered and treated as war heroes in New York City. But in Missouri the 9th Cavalry was 'unkindly and sneeringly received,' as recorded by Prioleau, unable to sit at numerous restaurants, while white soldiers were warmly greeted and allowed to eat free of charge."[11] This double standard was observed throughout the southern states in particular during this time.

All four of the African-American regiments, the 9th and 10th Cavalry and the 24th and 25th Infantry, were in

Wright was the highest ranking African American officer during the Spanish-American War.

combat at San Juan Heights. Later in the war, they served in Puerto Rico and the Philippines. Looking back at his memories of African-American troops fighting on the Heights, Roosevelt praised them, "They did as well as any soldiers could possibly do."[12] Some of their individual stories are inspiring.

On July 1, 1898, Corporal Bivins of the 10th Cavalry operated a three man Hotchkiss mountain gun alone, wounded, as his fellow soldiers were pinned down under fire.[13] Bivins soon became a hero in both military and civilian newspapers. He later wrote of his Cuban experiences in the book *Under the Fire with Tenth Cavalry*, one of the earliest and most popular of the Spanish-American

This cavalry unit of African-American soldiers served in the Spanish-American War.

War accounts written by participating soldiers. As a sergeant, Bivins served six months in the Philippines in 1901.

Sergeant Mingo Sanders was partially blinded when the 25th Infantry came under heavy fire at El Caney. Because of his exemplary record later in the Philippines, Colonel A. S. Burt, the regiment's commanding officer said, "Mingo Sanders is the best non-commissioned officer I have ever known."[14]

Of the 110 servicemen who earned the Medal of Honor during the war, six were African Americans. Five of these men were from the 10th Cavalry, a regiment that sent fewer than 500 men to Cuba. Four were privates who on June 30 volunteered to go ashore under fire during the battle of Tayacoba to rescue wounded after several previous attempts had failed.[15] On July 1, at Santiago Sergeant Major Edward L. Baker left cover and under fire rescued a wounded comrade from drowning. The sixth was Navy fireman Robert Penn.

BATTLING NAVIES AND DISEASES

"THERE COULD BE NO DOUBT AS TO THE OUTCOME BUT I SHOULD NEVER HAVE BELIEVED THAT OUR CHIPS WOULD BE DESTROYED SO RAPIDLY."

—Excerpt from Admiral Pascual Cervera's report of the Naval Battle of Santiago de Cuba to the Spain Ministry of Marine, August 1898.

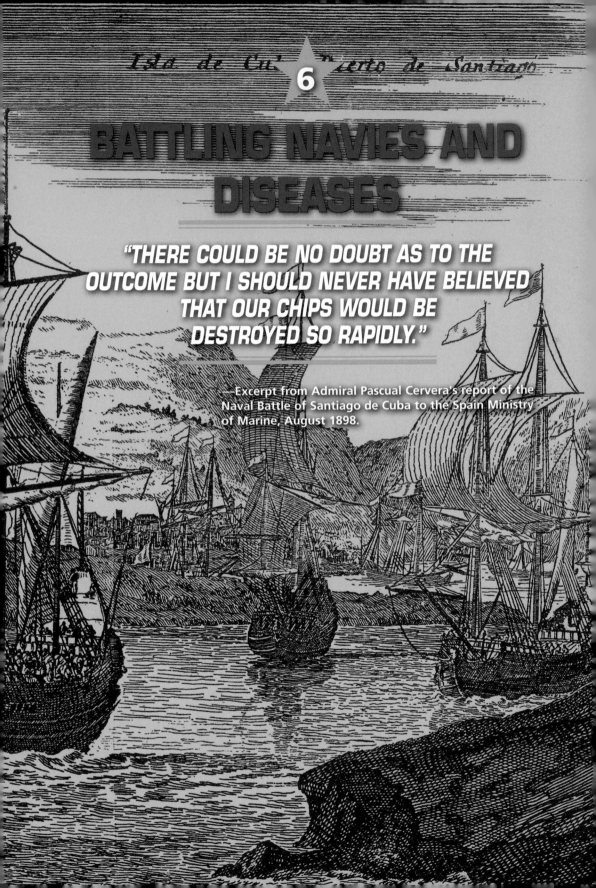

In the first days of the war, a squadron of Spanish ships left the Cape Verde Islands in the Atlantic Ocean on April 29, 1898. Admiral Pascual Cervera, Spain's chief naval officer, was bringing the squadron to Cuba. Three armored cruisers weighed in at seven-thousand-ton: the *Almirante Oquendo*, *Infanta Maria Teresa*, and *Vizcaya*, each heavily armed. The *Cristobal Colón* was a similar size but carried different armaments. The squadron included three small but feisty torpedo-boat destroyers, which were more maneuverable.

This drawing shows the naval battle at Santiago de Cuba, as Cervera attempts to escape the harbor.

As strong as the force seemed, there were weaknesses. American naval experts would later point out that all these ships lacked the heavier modern guns that had become available by 1898. Also, their ships were slowed by the weight of armor that was older and heavier than new steel alloys. In recent years, Spain had suffered hard economic times. Spanish armed forces had not been modernized and re-equipped.

The American naval commander, Admiral William J. Sampson, learned that Cervera's squadron would sail in less than two days. He steamed for Puerto Rico, which seemed a likely destination for the Spanish ships. Sampson's force of two battleships, three cruisers, and one torpedo boat could outgun the Spaniards, and the Admiral hoped for battle in the open sea.

The cunning Cervera slipped his fleet into the port of Santiago de Cuba instead, eluding the Americans. The Spanish ships were protected there by the heavy guns on the shore. Sampson's ships became tied up in blockade duty, keeping the Spanish fleet locked in the harbor.

The harbor entrance at Santiago de Cuba was narrow. Large ships had to follow a deep-water channel only 200 feet (61 m) wide at one point. The Americans devised a daring plan to keep the Spanish fleet bottled up in the harbor.

Hobson's Choice

The Americans realized that if a ship could be deliberately sunk in the narrows, the channel leading out of the Santiago de Cuba Harbor would be blocked. A single cruiser patrolling outside the harbor could drive off any Spanish crew attempting to reopen the passage.

Richmond P. Hobson, a specialist in naval construction, was chosen to lead a party of seven Americans on this mission. They were to sail an old but heavy coal ship, the *Merrimac,* into the narrows and deliberately sink it there. On June 3, a night with no moonlight, Hobson tried to sneak the *Merrimac* into the channel.

This was a daring mission. A small boat, a catamaran, was carried aboard the *Merrimac* to provide an escape vehicle after the sinking. One blast from Spanish guns could send both the catamaran and its crew to the bottom of Santiago de Cuba Harbor.

The old coal ship moved in darkness and silence, at first eluding the Spanish shore guns. Hobson said, "It was about three o'clock in the morning when we entered the channel and steamed in under the guns of the castle. The stillness of death prevailed. It was so dark we could scarcely see the headland."

"The silence was broken by the sound of a small picket boat approaching. She fired several shots from what seemed to be 3-pounder guns. The *Merrimac's* rudder was carried away by this fire."

"The run up the channel was very exciting. The picket boat gave the alarm and soon the guns of the ships and shore batteries were trained on us. Submarine mines and torpedoes also were exploded all about us. We could feel the ship tremble. Darkness saved us from utter destruction. The men launched the catamaran while I touched off the explosives to sink the ship."[1]

At the same instant, two torpedoes struck the *Merrimac.* It was "lifted out of the water and almost torn asunder."[2]

The tide was flowing into the harbor. The Americans in the catamaran could make no headway out to sea. A Spanish boat picked them up at about five o'clock in the morning and took them prisoner.

By daylight, they could see the results of the mission. The coal ship had been sunk in the channel, but pointing the wrong way. It had not responded to its rudder, making it impossible to steer. The *Merrimac* lay lengthwise, not crosswise, in the channel. Spanish ships could sail past its wreckage. The Americans consoled themselves by saying that now the Spaniards could not risk the narrowed channel at night.

Hobson and his men were imprisoned in a dungeon in the harbor castle. He wondered how they "were able to survive such terrible captivity."[3] They were still in their cells later when Admiral Sampson bombarded the harbor. For a time, they feared that the whole castle, including the dungeons, might be destroyed by American fire.

When the American Army surrounded Santiago de Cuba, the Spaniards released the prisoners. They made their way through the battle lines and were hailed as heroes when they finally reached the American side.

The Spanish Challenge the Blockade

A naval standoff continued. The Spaniards did not dare leave the harbor; the Americans continued their blockade. Admiral Sampson focused searchlights on the channel at night, not trusting the wrecked coal ship to halt the enemy.

Then, the seemingly safe harbor suddenly became dangerous for the Spaniards. The

The Flying Squadron *implemented the blockade of Cuba.*

American Army had seized the high ground at San Juan. It looked certain that they would soon capture the forts at the Santiago de Cuba harbor. The Spanish fleet would be trapped.

Admiral Cervera decided to make a run for it. Knowing he was outmatched, he tried to keep his escape plan secret. Commodore Winfield S. Schley, second in command of the American fleet, later said, "I knew of Cervera's proposed move twenty-four hours ahead."[4]

Early on July 3, Admiral Sampson sailed in his flagship to meet with General Shafter. The two officers were to plan a combined attack on Santiago de Cuba.

Sampson was about 5 miles (8 km) away when the Spanish flagship *Infanta Maria Teresa* was sighted emerging from Santiago de Cuba Harbor. Behind it, at 800-yard (731-m) intervals, came the *Vizcaya, Cristobal Colón*, and *Almirante Oquendo*. The Spanish squadron was making a desperate bid to escape. All four ships were firing heavy guns. Their shells went wide of the mark, sailing far above the Americans.

Commodore Schley, the senior American officer present, described what he saw:

> Our boys were waiting. The grim old vessels lay back like tigers waiting to pounce. Suddenly the whole Spanish fleet shot out of the channel. It was the grandest spectacle I ever witnessed. The flames were pouring out of their funnels, and as it left the channel the fleet opened fire with every gun on board. Shells were raining around like hail.
>
> My first impression was that of a lot of maddened bulls, goaded to desperation, dashing at their tormentors. ... The engagement must have lasted three hours, but I hardly knew what time was. I remember crashing holes through the Maria Teresa and giving chase to the Colón.[5]

Commodore Schley ordered his flagship, the *Brooklyn*, to starboard, which means a turn to the right. This created a break in the line of American ships, and the Spanish *Cristobal Colón* slipped past almost undamaged. Meanwhile, the *Infanta Maria Teresa* and *Almirante Oquendo* had caught American fire. Admiral Sampson, hearing the booming of heavy guns, was steaming back on the *New York* to join the battle. Two of the burning Spanish cruisers ran aground a few miles west of the harbor. The *Vizcaya* managed to make it a little farther but was burning fiercely. It ran ashore in flames. It hauled down its colors, and American ships sailed close to try to save its crew.

Commodore Schley, starting a rescue operation to help 1,200 to 1,500 Spanish sailors, approached the burning wreck of the *Vizcaya.* He said, "I lowered my boats to assist the unfortunate men who were being drowned by dozens or roasted on the burning decks. I soon discovered that Cuban rebels on the shore would not allow the struggling Spaniards to reach land. I put an immediate stop to this... but I could not stop the sharks." Schley said his rescue boats "had an inch or two of blood in the bottom."[6] Losses to the Spanish Navy were horrible. The American *Iowa*, which rescued many wounded, was "awash in blood."[7]

The *Cristobal Colón* raced 6 miles (9.6 km) ahead of American pursuit. But soon it came within reach of guns firing at a distance of about 9,000

This photograph captures the explosion of Spanish ship Vizcaya *during the Battle of Santiago de Cuba.*

yards (8,000 m). It, too, surrendered, running aground near a river mouth.

The battle was over. The entire Spanish squadron had been destroyed. The Spanish claimed to have suffered over five hundred casualties. But descriptions of the battle by eyewitnesses suggest that this figure should be doubled at least.

On the American side, no ship was heavily damaged, one sailor was dead, and only ten were wounded—but the American victory had been full of tense moments.

A Pause in Cuba

The Spanish Atlantic fleet could no longer bring men and supplies to Cuba from Spain. Furthermore, much of the Spanish Army in Cuba had been either destroyed or bottled up in the siege at Santiago de Cuba.

It was clear that the Americans could seize Santiago de Cuba by assault whenever they chose to, or then could destroy the city with heavy gunfire. Since that would mean the destruction of the Spanish forces, the rest of the island could then be taken quickly.

General Shafter, Admiral Sampson, and other commanders were not eager to carry out another attack and risk more losses. They could afford to wait for a peace settlement. Santiago de Cuba would have to surrender soon, anyway.

The Americans began to look beyond Cuba to other Spanish territories. The time had come to carry the war to more distant places. If the army stayed here, more deaths would come, but not from battle.

Death by Disease

Yellow fever was a greater enemy than the Spanish troops. Many diseases took their toll in the American camps. The most feared was Yellow fever, with a mortality rate up to 85 percent.

While no one in 1898 knew exactly how Yellow fever spread, people suspected low, damp ground to be a cause. This belief was not unreasonable, as mosquitoes can carry the disease and they breed in damp swamps and ponds. As soon as the victory at Santiago was done, by July 4 General William Shafter wrote to the Secretary of War, urging him to allow the Fifth Army Corps to move away from the city to higher ground, where the army surgeons felt the risk of disease would be less.

Although there was no more fighting in Cuba, the officials in Washington were hesitant about bringing the American Army home. Weeks went by with no action.

In Cuba, General Shafter summoned all his officers to a meeting to discuss health problems. Malaria, yellow fever, and typhoid were known to be rampant in Cuba during the summer season, and now the weather was growing increasingly hotter and wetter every day. It was a wise time to leave Cuba.

A letter of protest would have to be written to the highest authorities. The army officers, however, worried about their future careers if they wrote a complaint. Everyone present signed a letter composed by Theodore Roosevelt. To force the Secretary of War to act, Roosevelt leaked the letter to the Associated Press.

The Round Robin Letter, so called because of all the signatures, angered President McKinley and enraged Secretary of War Russell Alger. The secretary struck back by publishing private letters that Roosevelt had written to him, bragging about the Rough Riders. Although McKinley scowled and Alger fumed, within three days Shafter was ordered to send his healthy troops sailing for Montauk, New York. The action in Cuba was over.

Troopers who had already fallen ill were sent to Siboney hospital. There, the 24th Infantry was sent to assist nurses and doctors in caring for the sick. Their experience contradicted the popular belief that African-Americans had "special immunity" to tropical diseases.[8] In 40 days, malaria and yellow fever killed more than a third of the regiment's 460 men.

Relatively few men died in combat during the few weeks of the Spanish-American War in Cuba. After the *Maine* exploded, 968 American soldiers were killed in action. The total number of deaths was much higher, however. Disease killed over 5,000 soldiers.[9] Soldiers and nurses who died of yellow fever, malaria, and typhoid fever during the conflict were war casualties as much as those who died of wounds taken in battle.

AMERICANS TURN TO SPAIN'S NEW WORLD ISLANDS

"WE COULD NOT LEAVE THEM TO THEMSELVES— THEY WERE UNFIT FOR SELF-GOVERNMENT—AND THEY WOULD SOON HAVE ANARCHY AND MISRULE WORSE THAN SPAIN'S WAS..."

—President William McKinley giving reasons for the United States to keep the Philippines

After the two victories in Cuba, Americans turned their attention to other Spanish island possessions, especially to Puerto Rico and the Philippines.

In Cuba, many Americans felt that they were rescuing people who had already been rebelling against a cruel European government. There could be no such reasoning or excuse for the conquest of Puerto Rico. The island was at peace. But since the United States was already at war with Spain, it seemed logical to many Americans to seize Spanish possessions.

San Juan is marked in red on this map of Puerto Rico.

Also, the victories in Cuba had so delighted Americans that they were in no mood to object strongly about further American expansion.

Puerto Rico, which is about three times the size of Rhode Island, was first seen by Europeans in 1493, when Columbus arrived. Although it had a large native population, Columbus claimed it for the Spanish Crown. The explorer stayed only briefly, then sailed on to the larger island of Santo Domingo, now called Hispaniola.

On his second voyage to the Americas, Columbus brought Spaniards with him, who founded a colony on Santo Domingo. Fifteen more years passed before the Spanish nobleman Juan Ponce de Leon came to Puerto Rico from Santo Domingo in 1508.

He discovered the beautiful bay now known as San Juan Harbor. It was such a good harbor, and the land around it was so lush, that the explorer named it *Puerto Rico*, or "rich port" in English. Eventually the whole island, not just the harbor, was called that. Later, English-speaking people were puzzled by the Spanish spelling and shifted it to "Porto Rico." Congress changed the name back to the Spanish version in 1932.

Early Spanish colonists began exploring the island for gold, without much success. The natives of the island were of a group called Borinquen Indians, peaceful farmers related to the native people of North America and Central America. They welcomed the Spanish strangers. It is uncertain how large the population was. The largest estimate is over half a million people.

The Spanish, eager to acquire gold, enslaved the natives and forced them to work hard in mining attempts. Many of the Borinquen Indians died toiling in the tropical sun, digging in the hills, or washing gravel in streams. Others escaped, becoming enemies of the Spaniards. War and further enslavement followed. In 1582, the last surviving native died as a slave.

Having killed off the natives, the Spaniards imported Africans to replace them. Despite forced labor, the island did not prosper. Hurricanes destroyed plantations; warlike Carib people from other islands raided the colony; and eventually, English, Dutch, and French pirates attacked.

The Spaniards built forts at the harbor to repel pirate raids, including a landing by the English privateer Sir Francis Drake. Eventually, the pirates left the Caribbean. For awhile, there was peace.

Puerto Rico continued to be a Spanish colony. Impressive churches and public buildings were constructed. San Juan became a large city and so did San Germán, the island's second-largest town, although it was completely burnt by the French during one attempted invasion.

The island became highly aware of the war between Spain and the United States in May 1898, when Admiral Sampson appeared off San Juan searching for a Spanish fleet. No Spanish warships were to be found, but American forces fired some heavy guns at the castle guarding the harbor. This did almost no damage, and Sampson sailed away.

American ground forces landed on the southern part of the island on July 25, under command of General Nelson A. Miles. The first landing place not only surprised the Spaniards, but the Americans as well. Miles was supposed to be going to a port called Fajardo. On his second day at sea, he suddenly changed his mind and headed for a different place, Guánica, a small town at the opposite end of the island. Russell Alger, secretary of the Navy, learned of the change only when he read the newspapers the next day. He rushed frantically to redirect supplies and reinforcements.

Among the first troops to arrive were some Rough Riders, who had been stranded in Tampa when General Shafter limited their regiment's transport to Cuba. One said, "We thought that we would at last get to Cuba, better late than never. It was not to be. We sailed to Puerto Rico, trying to cheer ourselves up with the hope of a good fight there."[1] For the time being, these eager warriors were disappointed. They landed with no fight at all—except against rough waves and rocking boats.

The people of Puerto Rico had no intention of fighting a war with the Americans. They neither helped nor hindered the American invasions, but stayed carefully neutral as the Spanish Army retreated into the hills and jungles.

American troops occupied the entire south coast of the island with no resistance. Opposition came only when the US army moved northward into rougher country. "It was mostly snipers among the trees," said one soldier. "We never saw anything like an army."[2]

The first major town to be taken was Ponce. In a naval attack before the troops entered, four Americans were killed. The small Spanish garrison retreated north.

After quite a grand entrance into the town,

Here members of the 5th US Cavalry hide behind their horses as they keep watch for the Spanish Army in Puerto Rico.

General Miles summoned the residents of Ponce and made a speech. He said that he had come to liberate the people of Puerto Rico and give them the advantages of his enlightened civilization. In reality, the residents had been civilized for several centuries and were not seeking liberation.

General Miles planned a four-pronged operation to subdue the entire island. He mapped a 70-mile (113-km) advance along a good road to reach San Juan, the capital. Meanwhile, naval vessels were standing off the coast. The American warship *Newark*, with supporting vessels, bombarded the port of Manzanillo.

Miles encountered some Spanish skirmishers as he moved closer to San Juan. The other three troop columns also moved ahead, facing little opposition. There was never a real battle or siege.

On August 12, word reached the island that the American and Spanish governments had signed an armistice. Total American casualties included three dead and forty wounded while Spanish casualties were about ten times as great. The conquest of Puerto Rico was over and America held control. The people resumed their daily lives, having been little disturbed by the war.

Action in the Pacific

Admiral Dewey's sailors in the Philippines had been left holding a small strip of land after the American naval victory at Manila Bay. On May 7, 1889, Dewey sent a telegraph to Washington, DC, to report that he controlled the bay completely and could take the city of Manila at any time if additional troops were sent.[3]

America really did not know anything about these Pacific islands. It was said that even President McKinley had to look at a globe of the world before he could identify them.

Major General Wesley Merritt was given command of the U.S. Navy's Pacific operation. On May 25, he sent Brigadier General T. M. Anderson out from San Francisco with 2,491 men. This seemed like hardly more than a gesture, since Anderson said he needed 14,000 soldiers to do the job in the Philippines. Later, he changed his mind and asked for 20,000.

Meanwhile, the U.S. Army was scrambling to find men to send to Asia. Gradually soldiers were assembled, until at last 11,000 were dispatched to the faraway islands.

On June 20, on the first ships sailing east, Anderson paused long enough to seize the island of Guam, a Spanish possession in the western Pacific Ocean some 5,000 miles (8,046 km) off the coast of Hawaii. The U.S. Navy wanted this small island for a supply base at the edge of the Western Pacific. There was no resistance at Guam, once the puzzled governor understood what was happening. No one had warned him to expect an American landing.

On June 30, Anderson's troops arrived in Manila Bay and joined Dewey's occupying force. Within another month there were 11,000 American troops at Manila, and another 5,000 on the way across the Pacific. Admiral Dewey and General Merritt were ready to begin the conquest of the Philippines.

A Briefly Independent Nation of Islands

In one respect, the Philippines were like Cuba. Both Spanish colonies had vigorous movements for independence, and both had been in rebellion long before Americans arrived on the scene.

The Philippine Islands were not a united country. Filipinos lived scattered among more than 7,000 islands. They spoke several different languages and followed differing religious teachings. Still, a longing for an independent nation was slowly asserting itself, especially among the well-educated younger generation there.

The first violence of the independence movement took place in 1872. Two hundred soldiers—Filipinos in the service of Spain—mutinied and raised the cry of independence at Cavite Arsenal. After their revolt failed, the Spaniards dealt out executions and long prison sentences to the rebels.

A full-scale revolution exploded in 1896, centered in Cavite province on Luzon, the largest of the islands and the site of Manila. Among the leaders was Emilio Aguinaldo.

Although the fighting between Spaniards and Filipinos was far from over, the rebels declared independence on June 12, 1898. Aguinaldo would be the country's first president. On that date, the

American invasion fleet was sailing between San Francisco and Guam. When the Americans landed in the Philippines, war was already raging there. Even earlier, when Dewey entered Manila Bay, the Philippine capital was already under partial siege by rebels.

People in the United States looked upon Filipino affairs as a remote mystery. They seemed uninterested in islands half a world away. Besides, the Filipinos were racially and religiously different from most Americans. Anti-Asiatic prejudice was widespread in the United States at the end of the nineteenth century.[4]

The American government ordered its commanders in the islands to avoid cooperation with Aguinaldo and his rebels.[5] While the American government had agreed for the Cubans to have independence, it was opposed to the same idea in the Philippines. No such thing was announced by the McKinley administration until much later, and nothing about the two different policies appeared in American newspapers at the time. But orders and actions showed there was one standard for Cuba and another for the islands of the Philippines.

The Fall of Manila

Aguinaldo was not happy about the arrival of the Americans. He had plans to capture Manila with his own army. General Anderson reported that the Filipino leader seemed suspicious and not at all friendly.[6] Anderson established a landing place he named Camp Dewey. It was 3 miles (5 km) from

Dewey's flagship Olympia *engages with the enemy in the Battle of Manila Bay.*

Manila and just behind the lines of the rebel army, which was already besieging the city.

The Spanish Army holding Manila had 13,000 soldiers centered in what was known as "Old Manila." This large part of the city was practically a fortress. The Pasig River protected the north side. Blockhouses, walls, and trenches defended the other three sides.

The city was short of food and water. Also, the reports of Spanish defeats in Cuba and the sinking of Spanish ships had weakened morale. Thousands of rebels encircled the city, and now a large American Army had arrived.

General Merritt, the chief commander, arrived just before the end of July and announced a purely American attack on Manila. He wanted to ignore the rebels. This was difficult, for they were everywhere. He had to deal with them, but he kept his cooperation with them to a minimum.

Merritt and Dewey sent a joint message to the Spanish commander, General Fermin Jaudenes. Unless he surrendered, they would bombard the city from both land and sea, then assault it. After delays and messages back and forth, the Americans attacked on August 13. The Spaniards could have put up a strong, but doomed, resistance. Wisely, they surrendered after only a token defense.

The war against Spain in the Philippines was over. America had suffered losses of 20 killed, plus 105 men reported wounded. The United States had conquered a land that was a little larger than the state of Colorado. They had only conquered it on paper, though. In reality, the Filipino people would soon have more to say about the matter.

The End of the War

On August 12, 1898, the United States and Spain agreed to a cease-fire. Almost four months would pass before a final agreement between the two countries was reached. What became known as the Treaty of Paris was concluded on December 10. Diplomatic formalities and details would drag on until the following April, eight months after hostilities actually ended.

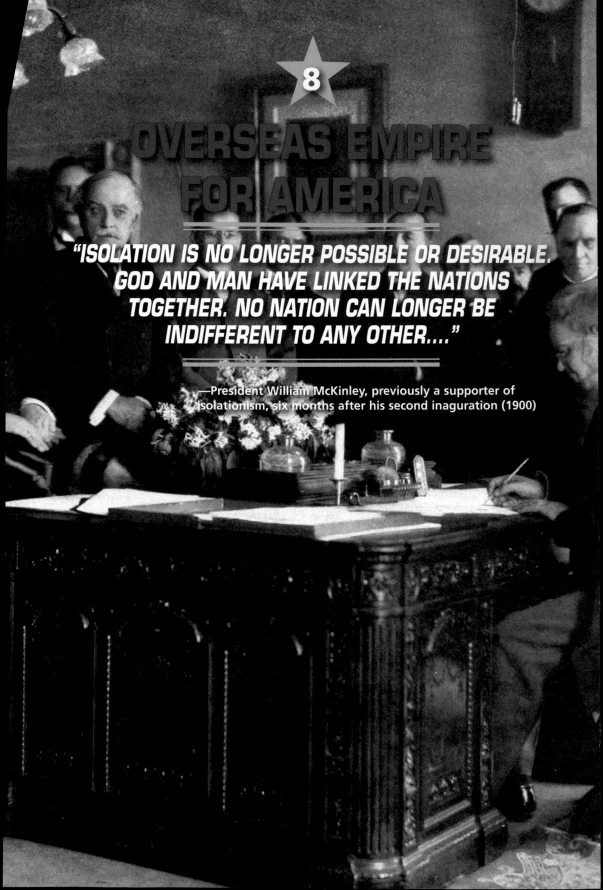

8

OVERSEAS EMPIRE FOR AMERICA

"ISOLATION IS NO LONGER POSSIBLE OR DESIRABLE. GOD AND MAN HAVE LINKED THE NATIONS TOGETHER. NO NATION CAN LONGER BE INDIFFERENT TO ANY OTHER...."

—President William McKinley, previously a supporter of isolationism, six months after his second inaguration (1900)

Secretary of State John Hay and many others grappled with the process of creating the Treaty of Paris with Spain. In the end, Spain agreed to grant Cuba independence, give Puerto Rico and Guam to the United States, and sell the Philippines to the United States for $20 million. During that time, Hawaii was made an American territory. Fighting in the Philippines went on. It seemed that the U.S. War Department found it easier to get into a war than to end one.

Jingoes in Congress were shouting their demands for an American empire. More cautious Americans warned against too much participation in worldwide affairs. Slowly and angrily, compromises were made.

Cuba After the War

Cuba's independence was the easiest matter to settle. Before the war began, Congress had declared that America would not seize the island. This had been agreed to in the Treaty of Paris, which ended the war in 1898. Yet American jingoes resisted letting Cuba go. Politicians who wanted to build an empire belittled the long and bitter struggle the Cubans had waged to have their own nation. American troops continued to occupy the island until 1902, with Leonard Wood appointed as Governor-General.

These American troops did much to improve public health in Cuba. Yellow fever had long been a problem there. Walter Reed, an American army surgeon serving in Havana, explained that mosquitoes spread the deadly disease. In a joint effort with Cubans, the army helped control the population of disease-spreading insects. In other projects, clinics were founded and water supplies were made safer. Army engineers also helped with rebuilding the war-torn country. When the American troops left in 1902, they held on to only the Guantánamo naval base in Cuba.

An Unsteady Course

In 1902, Congress adopted the Platt Amendment and required Cuba to include its provisions in the Cuban constitution. This law attached major conditions to Cuban independence. Strict limitations were placed on the ability of the Cuban government to borrow money. Cuba would have to lease naval stations to the United States and continue health and sanitation projects started by the American Army.

More important and aggravating to Cubans was the claim that America had a right to interfere in Cuban affairs whenever it thought necessary. One Cuban journalist wrote, "The Americans have made our country free. As free as a dog on a leash."[1] This statement had more than a grain of truth. American financial interests controlled much of Cuba with heavy investments, especially in the sugar industry and the rum distillation industry. Later, Americans would also put money into tourist resorts.

Cuban democracy followed an unsteady course. After four years of calm and prosperity, the first Cuban president, Tomas Estrada Palma, faced widespread revolt after an election marked by fraud and violence. He appealed to the United States to intervene since the island was in disorder. Estrada Palma resigned in 1908, and in September of that year American troops landed. The rebellion halted, a temporary government was set up, and American soldiers left on April 1, 1909.

A republic modeled on the United States struggled to improve conditions for four years. Then American troops, this time Marines, returned in 1912 when what has been called a "race war" broke out.[2] African-Cuban sugarcane workers had revolted against plantation owners, many of whom were Americans and Europeans. The impoverished condition of farm workers in Cuba was a recurring problem. Although Americans intervened in Cuban affairs in many ways, they avoided the basic problem of workers' rights. Poor people in Cuba remained in terrible poverty and lacked education.

In the years between 1912 and 1933, Cuba enjoyed a few periods of peace and prosperity broken by years of economic depression and political unrest, often bringing riots and general strikes. The Platt Amendment was revoked in 1932, but America kept a naval base at Guantánamo Bay. After an especially bloody revolt in 1933, a military leader, Colonel Carlos Mendieta, was proclaimed president of Cuba by most of the quarreling groups on the island. The United States promptly recognized his government.

Colonel Mendieta gave broad powers to his chief of staff, General Fulgencio Batista. Soon Batista seized the government. When students and workers revolted against the repeated postponement of elections, Batista suppressed the uprising harshly, openly becoming the dictator of Cuba. The United States now recognized his government. The years 1934 through 1959 were marked by corruption and tyranny. Cuban officials, led by Batista, were often partners with international gangsters and crime bosses. Freedom of speech and press were denied on the island, while police brutality broke up workers' strikes and protests.

In 1959, a young military officer named Fidel Castro took power through armed revolt. Castro, the son of a prominent Cuban family, headed a band of revolutionary guerrillas who were driven from Cuba. Regrouping his forces in Mexico, a country hostile to the dictator Batista, Castro returned to Cuba with a small force. This time he triumphed, with the support of a large majority of the Cuban people.

The bearded Castro, usually photographed in a rumpled army uniform, was at first hailed by Cubans and many Americans as the restorer of Cuban democracy. But Prime Minister Castro soon suppressed the Cuban constitution. Thousands of his political opponents fled the island, most seeking refuge in Florida.

In April 1961, Cuban exiles supported by the United States attempted to invade their homeland. They were defeated in a struggle known as the Bay of Pigs. Fidel Castro sought military and economic support from the Soviet Union. In exchange he sent Cuban soldiers to aid Soviet-sponsored war in Africa and Soviet-backed revolutionary efforts in Latin America. America denounced Castro's political system as communism and sharply limited trade and travel between the United States and Cuba.

Fidel Castro was a socialist and revolutionary who governed Cuba from 1959 to 2008.

Cuban Missile Crisis

Hostility reached a danger point in October 1962 during the Cuban Missile Crisis. America learned the Soviet Union had installed missiles in Cuba, after Cuban leaders became convinced that the United States was planning to attack. The missiles were in range to launch nuclear attacks on American cities. American officials blockaded the island to stop further shipment of Soviet arms. During this time, an American spy plane was also shot down over Cuba.[4] The ships from the Soviet Union soon withdrew.

The Soviet Union offered to remove the missiles if the United States would promise not to invade Cuba. It later said that it would not remove the missiles unless the United States dismantled American military bases in Turkey, an American ally bordering the Soviet Union. President John F. Kennedy agreed publicly to the first Soviet proposal, but also sought a private agreement to remove U.S. nuclear missiles from Turkey in exchange for the removal of Soviet missiles from Cuba. On October 28, Soviet leader Nikita Khrushchev accepted Kennedy's offer, ending the crisis. Nuclear war was narrowly averted, not only by diplomacy but a Soviet officer's courage.[3] Vasili Alexandrovich Arkhipov, one of three senior officers on Soviet submarine B-59 as it was battered by American navy depth charges, refused to launch the submarine's nuclear weapon.

As the Century Turns

In 1990, the collapse of the Soviet Union lost the Castro government the support it had been receiving. The Castro regime has often been denounced by American leaders as communist. Communism is an economic system in which all means of production—land, mines, factories, railroads, and businesses—are owned by the people, private property does not exist, and all goods and services are shared equally.

Fidel Castro ordinarily used the word "socialist" to describe the system he directed as president. Socialism is an economic system in which the factors of production are owned by the public and operate for the welfare of all. Some Latin American and Canadian journalists who have studied Cuba agree that the government is in many ways socialist, with some communist ideals, and is mostly a system devised from year to year by the Castro regime. The regime has been successful in increasing literacy and food production, and improving medical care for most Cubans. Castro delegated his presidential duties to his brother Raúl Castro in 2006. The National Assembly unanimously voted Raúl Castro to the presidency in 2008.

A Different Role for Puerto Rico

Unlike Cuba and the Philippines, Puerto Rico had no strong movement for independence from Spain at the time of the Spanish-American War. The United States annexed the island in 1898.

After other attempts to govern Puerto Rico, Congress passed the Jones Act in 1917. This act granted American citizenship to Puerto Ricans and allowed some measure of self-government. But the problems of the overcrowded island were far from solved. Natural disasters such as hurricanes have plagued Puerto Rico. Its exports, including sugar, coffee, rum, and fruits, often suffer from unfavorable world economic conditions. Recently, light industries such as needlework and plastic products have grown.

Some hardships have been relieved by emigration to the mainland United States. Many emigrants have kept close ties to their homeland, and some return to Puerto Rico annually. Many maintain strong traditions of language, religion, family, and social customs.

In national elections, Puerto Ricans have solidly rejected both independence from the United States and a proposal for statehood within the United States. Yet a small but strong movement for independence has existed for decades. The island remains a largely self-governing territory of the United States.

Adding Hawaii to the American Empire

The Hawaiian Islands were not at stake in the Spanish-American War, as they were not controlled by Spain. However, they became part of the United States as a by-product of the conflict.

These inhabited Pacific islands were named the Sandwich Islands by explorer James Cook, for an English nobleman, the Earl of Sandwich. In 1803, Hawaii was recognized by Britain as an independent kingdom. Queen Liliuokalani was overthrown in 1893 by a republic that was in part controlled by American business interests. Its first president was S. B. Dole, whose name many Americans recognize from his family's business, Dole Pineapple.

The so-called "democratic" government was largely in the hands of foreign plantation owners and food exporters— most of them Americans. American-Christian missionaries were also prominent in the islands.

The United States annexed Hawaii at the request of this legislature in 1898. This act was in keeping with the empire-building spirit. Hawaii's fine harbors afforded excellent supply stations for American ships bound for Asia.

At the time of annexation, there was some talk on the floor of Congress about possible statehood for Hawaii, like Alaska. Some members of Congress ridiculed the idea, insisting that Hawaiian representatives in Washington, DC, would address the Senate in broken English with Chinese accents while wearing long braided pigtails.[5] This prejudice against Asian people was a sign of how some Americans regarded the Philippines as well. Suspicion and dislike for Asians, nicknamed "the yellow peril," was strong in the United States.

Hawaii became the fiftieth state of the American union in 1959. Contrary to some opinions expressed years earlier, Hawaii today ranks among the highest of American states in education, health, and welfare. Barack Obama, the 44th American President, was born there.

War in the Philippines: Forgotten in America

As soon as the Filipino people stopped fighting the Spaniards for independence, they started fighting the Americans for the same reason. Not long after his arrival in the Philippine Islands, General T. M. Anderson remarked, "I have underrated the natives. They are not ignorant, savage tribes, but have a civilization of their own."[6] Admiral Dewey agreed with him: "They are more capable of self-government than the people of Cuba."[7]

Americans, for the most part, did not share these opinions. Filipinos were Asian, so they were not to be trusted. In negotiations with Spain, an American diplomat expressed the opinion that Filipinos might have independence gradually as they "become civilized and Christianized."[8]

Most Americans had traveled very little at that time. They knew next to nothing about Asian people. Belief in what British poet Rudyard Kipling called "The White Man's Burden" was popular. This "burden" was the supposed duty of members of the white race to care for and lead conquered people of other races. The idea was based on a very self-satisfied belief in European superiority. The carriers of this "burden" always seemed to make profits, gain services, and command others.

It quickly became clear that Americans did not trust Filipinos to manage their own affairs. A smaller number of Americans saw potential profits from trade and business in Asia. The Philippines had products, raw materials, and markets that were useful for American enterprise. Jingoes and certain businessmen had no intention of letting these islands slip away. During this same period American newspapers continued to chastise European powers for their imperialism. The Second Boer War was especially unpopular, and soured Anglo-American relations. The anti-imperialist press would often draw parallels between the U.S. in the Philippines and the British in the Second Boer War.

While Admiral Dewey remained in the Philippines, he punished soldiers who tortured captives during interrogation. After he returned to the United States in 1899, some atrocities were reported on both sides. In 1900, 56,000 American troops were sent to the Philippines to suppress Filipino independence fighters.[9] Among these troops were the African American regiments, the 24th and 25th Infantry, and the 9th and 10th Cavalry. As many as 200,000 Filipinos died from hunger, disease, gunfire, and brutality in the next two years. Leading rebels caught by Americans were hanged.

Not all Americans were in favor of this action. Famous Americans such as author Samuel Clemens spoke powerfully against the war in the islands.[10] Surgeon and Civil War veteran Jerome R. Riley formed the National Negro Anti-Expansion, Anti-Imperialist, Anti-Trust, and Anti-Lynching League, in opposition to American imperialism.

American Defectors

During 1899 –1902, a total of twenty African American soldiers defected to the Filipino revolutionary army led by Emilio Aguinaldo. The most well-known of these was David Fagen, of the 24th Infantry. A laborer before he enlisted in 1898, Fagen saw combat when the 24th Infantry were sent to Manila in June 1899. In combat against Filipino patriots in Central Luzon, Fagen argued with his commanding officers. His requests for transfer were turned down. In November 1899, he defected to the Filipino revolutionary army and won their trust. Promoted to captain, Fagen served there two years, clashing at least eight times with American troops. He took a Filipina wife. When key Filipino leaders were captured in 1901, they tried to arrange an amnesty for Fagen. Instead, the Americans put out a reward for his capture. Fagen eluded a year-long manhunt before an indigenous hunter delivered a severed head for the bounty. In the Philippines, Fagen is remembered as a hero who resisted the injustice of imperialism.[11]

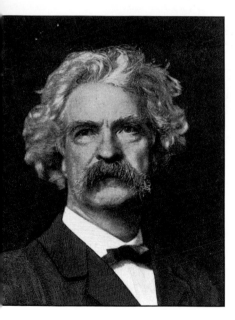

Samuel Clemens, also known as Mark Twain, was best known for his writing, which included The Adventures of Tom Sawyer *and* Adventures of Huckleberry Finn.

A Protectorate

On leaving Cuba in 1902, Leonard Wood went to the Philippines in command of the division and later the Department of the East. He served as governor of Moro province from 1903 to 1906. He was one of many military governors while the Philippines remained a protectorate.

In December 1941, at the beginning of World War II, Japanese armed forces invaded and occupied the islands for the next three years. Many Filipinos suffered greatly through the

Japanese occupation. In late 1944 through early 1945, General Douglas MacArthur led American troops to re-conquer the Philippines.

Independence was officially granted to the Philippines on July 4, 1946. Almost half a century had passed since the Filipino patriot Aguinaldo had surrounded the Spanish-held city of Manila with trenches, confident that his country would soon win freedom.

Presidential Material

Despite charges that Roosevelt was boastful and condescending, his political future was bright because of the war. He had curated his persona, becoming "the most famous man in America."[12] In 1898 he was elected governor of New York. The state Republicans didn't trust him, so encouraged him to run for vice president of the United States, then considered a prestigious but powerless role. When William McKinley was reelected to serve a second term as president, it was with Roosevelt as his running mate.

On September 6, 1901, McKinley was shot by an anarchist in Buffalo, New York, and died eight days later. Theodore Roosevelt then became the youngest president to that date. He championed his "Square Deal" domestic policies, and was re-elected in 1904.

His life crossed paths with Mingo Sanders once again. In Brownsville, Texas, the 25th Infantry was accused of a shooting incident. President Roosevelt sent officers to conduct an inquiry, who could find no witnesses. Roosevelt ordered the men to be given dishonorable discharges without any kind of trial, including Sergeant Sanders, the man who had shared food and a daring battle with him. He waited to order the discharges until November 7, 1906, one day after Congressional elections, so that black voters would not abandon the party.

The discharges were not forgotten in later years. President Taft appointed Sanders to federal positions as an anti-Roosevelt reminder. Still, the Roosevelt persona dominates history books. Roosevelt was posthumously awarded the Medal of Honor by President Bill Clinton in 2001, for the daring charge up San Juan Hill, a hundred years after the 109 other Medals of Honor earned during the Spanish-American War.

Theordore Roosevelt when he succeeded McKinley.

Further Study of the *Maine*

In 1975 and 1976, almost eighty years after the sinking of the *Maine*, U.S. Rear Admiral Hyman G. Rickover conducted a study to determine the specific cause. He was aided by various experts, including an engineer from Taylor Naval Ship Research and

Development Center and a physicist from the Naval Surface Weapons Center.

Several investigators had studied the *Maine* explosion before. The most thorough probe had been conducted by an official Board of Inquiry of the U.S. Navy in 1911. Rickover's experts used evidence gathered from this investigation, in addition to reports accumulated over the years. The second of two explosions close together was obviously the ship's magazine of ammunition. But what set it off?

Rickover's scientific team determined that the *Maine* sank due to an internal explosion. There had been a great deal of coal dust in the ship's hold. Air thick with coal dust is highly explosive. Blasts that occur at sea and on land have been traced to these dangerous conditions. Rickover's investigation decided that this was the best theory to explain the *Maine* explosion.

Later writers pointed out the *Maine* had taken on bituminous coal, which was more subject to spontaneous combustion in ships than anthracite coal. In 1998, the National Geographic society commissioned a computer analysis exploring the sinking of the *Maine*. The model suggested spontaneous combustion was easily possible, whereas a mine would have had to be detonated in precisely the right place.[13]

A Backward Look

The Spanish-American War lasted less than four months—114 days of hostilities.[14] The American

Army lost 29 officers and 440 soldiers in battle. Army deaths due to disease included 67 officers and 1,700 soldiers. The American Navy, which had fairly good sanitary conditions, lost 56 men to disease. These losses were small compared to all other American wars. During the undeclared war against the Sioux nation in 1876, Lieutenant Colonel George Custer lost more men in a single day at Little Bighorn than were lost in all the battles of the Spanish-American War.

The war set the United States on a road from which it has never turned back, although that road has zigzagged often. America, which before had tried to live more or less in isolation, was thrust powerfully into world affairs. In time, this position proved to be more costly and difficult than the leaders of America ever imagined in 1898.

The Spanish-American War did much to build American pride. It helped unite a country that had been torn apart by the Civil War a generation before. Above all, it taught the United States a lesson about finding its place in the world and becoming a major nation.

Chronology

February 24, 1895— In Cuba, an insurrection begins the Cuban War for Independence. Up to 25,000 rebels take arms during the next three years, while Spain sends over 200,000 armed reinforcements to Cuba.

June 12, 1895—US President Grover Cleveland declares American neutrality in the Cuban insurrection.

February 16, 1896—Valeriano Weyler becomes captain general in Cuba and orders thousands of Cubans herded into concentration camps under his reconcentration policy.

December 7, 1896—President Grover Cleveland declares limited patience with Spain's oppression of Cubans.

March 4, 1897—William McKinley inaugurated as President of the USA.

April 6, 1897—Theodore Roosevelt named assistant secretary of the Navy.

October 1897—**Spain** recalls Weyler and institutes reforms in the administration of Cuba, but rebels still struggle for independence.

December 6, 1897—President McKinley announces that many Cubans have died in government camps and threatens to intervene with force.

January 1898—During a riot by Cuban Spanish loyalists, four printing presses are destroyed. The US Consul-General telegraphs Washington DC about his fears for the safety of more than 8,000 Americans living in Cuba.

January 25, 1898—USS Maine arrives at Havana, Cuba, the

first American naval vessel to visit Cuba in over three years.

February 9, 1898—Personal letter by Spanish ambassador Enrique Dupuy de Lóme, criticizing McKinley, is published in the New York Journal newspaper.

February 15, 1898—In Havana Harbor, USS Maine is destroyed by an explosion.

March 1898—In response to a demand by President McKinley, the Cuban government ends the forced relocation of residents and offers negotiation with the independence fighters. The rebels refuse a truce.

March 17, 1898—Senator Redfield Proctor of Vermont shakes the U.S. Senate and many Americans with report on conditions in Cuba.

April 11, 1898—President McKinley asks Congress for the authority to use military force in Cuba against Spain.

April 22, 1898—U.S. Navy blockades Cuba.

April 24, 1898—Spain declares war on the United States.

April 25, 1898—Congress declares war on Spain, retroactive to April 21.

May 1, 1898—Commodore George Dewey destroys Spanish fleet in Manila Bay, Philippine Islands.

May 15, 1898— Lieutenant Colonel Theodore Roosevelt arrives in Texas to train with the Rough Riders under Colonel Wood.

June 10, 1898—First Marine Battalion under Huntington lands and secures Guantanamo Bay, Cuba.

June 22, 1898—General Shafter's troops begin landing at Daiquiri on the Cuban coast.

June 24, 1898—American and Spanish troops fight battle at Las Guasimas, Cuba.

July 1, 1898—American and Cuban troops take El Viso Fort, the town of El Caney, and San Juan Heights.

July 3, 1898—Spanish squadron attempts to run American blockade at Santiago de Cuba Harbor. Spanish ships destroyed.

July 8, 1898—Hawaii is acquired after the Hawaii annexation resolution is passed.

July 17, 1898—Spanish surrender city of Santiago de Cuba.

July 18, 1898—Colonel Leonard Wood is named military governor of Santiago de Cuba.

July 25, 1898—Americans invade Puerto Rico.

August 12, 1898—American and Spanish officials agree to a cease-fire.

August 13, 1898—Unaware of cease-fire, Admiral Dewey and General Wesley Merritt attack Manila. Spain surrenders Philippines.

August 14, 1898—General Wesley Merritt declares a military government in Manila, Philippines, with himself as the first military governor.

December 10, 1898—Treaty of Paris officially ends war. Spain agrees to grant Cuba independence, give Puerto Rico and Guam to the United States, and sell the Philippines to the United States for $20 million. Hawaii is made an American territory.

December 23, 1898—Guam is placed under the control of the US Navy.

January 17, 1899—USA claims Wake Island to use for a telegraph cable link to Philippines.

February 6, 1899—Treaty of Paris passes in the US Senate.

1900—Foraker Act allows some self-government in Puerto Rico.

1902—American forces withdraw from Cuba.

1917—Puerto Ricans become American citizens.

Chapter Notes

CHAPTER 1. HAVANA HARBOR EXPLOSION

1. Michael Blow, *A Ship to Remember* (New York: William Morrow & Co., 1992), p. 26.
2. Ibid., p. 38.
3. Ibid., p. 28.
4. George T. Grange, *The Authentic Life of President William McKinley* (Baltimore, Md.: Henderson Press, 1911), p. 62.
5. Ibid., p. 163.
6. Blow, p. 38.
7. Ibid.
8. Brad K. Berner, *The Spanish-American War: A Historical Dictionary* (Lanham, Md.: The Scarecrow Press, Inc., 1998), p. 308.
9. George B. Rea, *An American in Cuba* (New York: Hallam & Hart, 1903), p. 6.
10. Ibid., p. 7.
11. Ibid., p. 57.
12. Sylvester Scovel, *Cuba: Our Tragic Neighbor* (New York: Johnson and Massie, 1900), p. 44.
13. David Traxel, *1898: The Birth of the American Century* (New York: Alfred A. Knopf, 1998), p. 103.
14. Rodofo Sanchez, *La lucha larga de Cuba* (Mexico: Colegio de Mexico, 1954), p. 87.
15. Traxel, p. 103.
16. John Edward Weems, *The Fate of the* Maine (New York: Henry Holt and Company, 1958), p. 71.
17. Joseph Smith, *The Spanish-American War* (New York: Longman Publishers, 1994), p. 33.
18. Traxel, p. 105.
19. Weems, p. 90.
20. Blow, p. 102.

21. Weems, p. 92.
22. Traxel, p. 108.

CHAPTER 2. SLOGANS AND SUPPORT

1. Brad K. Berner, *The Spanish-American War: A Historical Dictionary* (Lanham, Md.: The Scarecrow Press, Inc., 1998), p. 314.
2. Ibid., p. 216.
3. Wayne H. Morgan, *America's Road to Empire: The War With Spain and Overseas Expansion* (New York: John Wiley and Sons, Inc., 1965), pp. 52–53.
4. Ibid.
5. Ibid., p. 53.
6. Rodofo Sanchez, *La lucha larga de Cuba* (Mexico: Colegio de Mexico, 1954), p. 152.
7. Sylvester Scovel, *Cuba: Our Tragic Neighbor* (New York: Johnson and Massie, 1900), p. 58.
8. Berner, p. 314.
9. Ibid., p. 171.
10. Sanchez, p. 161.
11. Edmund Morris, *The Rise of Theodore Roosevelt* (New York: Ballantine Books, 1980), p. 610.
12. David F. Trask, *The War With Spain in 1898* (New York: Macmillan, Co., Inc., 1981), p. 28.
13. Berner, p. 101.
14. Joseph Smith, *The Spanish-American War* (New York: Longman Publishers, 1994), p. 46.
15. Sanchez, p. 165.
16. Morgan, p. 23.
17. Sanchez, p. 156.
18. David Traxel, *1898: The Birth of the American Century* (New York: Alfred A. Knopf, 1998), p. 116.

19. George T. Grange, *The Authentic Life of President William McKinley* (Baltimore, Md.: Henderson Press, 1911), p. 195.
20. Ibid., p. 196.
21. Michael Blow, *A Ship to Remember* (New York: William Morrow & Co., 1992), p. 144.

CHAPTER 3.   A POPULAR WAR IN PUBLIC OPINION

1. Walter Millis, *The Martial Spirit: A Study of Our War with Spain* (Boston: Houghton Mifflin, Co., 1931), p. 162.
2. Joseph Smith, *The Spanish-American War* (New York: Longman Publishers, 1994), p. 83.
3. Ibid., p. 84.
4. Ibid., p. 97.
5. David Traxel, *1898: The Birth of the American Century* (New York: Alfred A. Knopf, 1998), p. 137.
6. Millis, p. 188.
7. Edmund Morris, *The Rise of Theodore Roosevelt* (New York: Ballantine Books, 1980), p. 578.
8. Fraser, Steve, The Age of Acquiesence: The Life and Death of American Resistance to Organized Wealth and Power, (New York, NY: Little, Brown & Co, 2015), p. 88.
9. Morris, p. 188.
10. Millis, p. 112.
11. G.J.A. O'Toole, *The Spanish-American War: An American Epic, 1898* (New York: W. W. Norton & Co., 1984), p. 137.

CHAPTER 4.   CAVALRY VOLUNTEERS AND VETERANS

1. Edmund Morris, *The Rise of Theodore Roosevelt* (New York: Ballantine Books, 1980), p. 614.
2. Virgil Carrington Jones, *Roosevelt's Rough Riders* (New York: Doubleday, 1971), p. 35.

3. Brad K. Berner, *The Spanish-American War: A Historical Dictionary* (Lanham, Md.: The Scarecrow Press, Inc., 1998), p. 321.
4. Morris, p. 620.
5. Ibid., p. 618.
6. Ibid., p. 624.
7. Ibid.
8. Ibid.
9. Ibid., p. 627.
10. Morris, p. 628.
11. Jones, p. 109.
12. Evelyn Cherpak, editor, *Three Splendid Little Wars: The Diary of Joseph K. Taussig,* (Newport, RI: Naval College Press, 2009) p. 10.
13. Graham A. Cosmas, *An Army for Empire* (Columbia: University of Missouri Press, 1971), p. 92.
14. Morris, p. 634.
15. Ibid., p. 635.
16. Jones, p. 100.

CHAPTER 5. COMBAT IN CUBA

1. J. R. Young, *Reminiscences and Thrilling Stories of the War by Returned Heroes* (Philadelphia: Standard, 1899), p. 44.
2. Edmund Morris, *The Rise of Theodore Roosevelt* (New York: Ballantine Books, 1980), p. 637.
3. Ibid.
4. Tiburcio P. Castaneda, *La explosion del* Maine *y la guerra de los Estados Unidos con Espana* (Habana: Prensa Atlas, 1925), p. 102.
5. Virgil Carrington Jones, *Roosevelt's Rough Riders* (New York: Doubleday, 1971), p. 136.
6. Morris, p. 650.

7. Ibid.

8. Charles Morton, "Concerning the Actions of the 3rd US Cavalry at the Battle of the San Juan Heights." *The Spanish American War Centennial Website*. Posted March 3, 2010. http://www.spanamwar.com /3rdUSCavalryMorton.htm

9. T. G. Steward, *Colored Regulars in the U.S. Army* (New York: Arno Press, 1969), p. 133.

10. Paul Matthews, "9th & 10th Cavalry Regiment." *Buffalo Soldiers National Museum* website. Updated 2014. http:// buffalosoldiermuseum.com/category/9th-10th-cavalry -regiment

11. Trevor Goodloe, "Prioleau, George 1856 – 1927." *BlackPast.org*. Updated 2015. http://www.blackpast.org /aaw/chaplain-george-prioleau-1856-1927

12. Steward, p. 133.

13. Howard Cabiao, "Bivins, Horace W. (1862 0 1937)." *BlackPast.org*. Updated 2015. http://www.blackpast.org /aah/bivans-horace-w-1862-1937

14. Harry Lembeck, "Sanders, Mingo (1857 – 1929)." *BlackPast.org*. Updated 2015. http://www.blackpast.org /aah/mingo-sanders-1857-1929

15. Frank Schubert, "Mickey". "10th Cavalry Regiment." *BlackPast.org* Updated 2015. http://www.blackpast.org /aaw/10th-cavalry-regiment-1866-1944

CHAPTER 6. BATTLING NAVIES AND DISEASES

1. J. R. Young, *Reminiscences and Thrilling Stories of the War by Returned Heroes* (Philadelphia: Standard, 1899), p. 87.

2. Ibid., p. 89.

3. Ibid., p. 93.

4. Tiburcio P. Castaneda, *La explosion del* Maine *y la guerra de los Estados Unidos con Espana* (Habana: Prensa Atlas, 1925), p. 178.

5. Young, p. 91.

6. Ibid., p. 92.

7. Ibid., p. 94.

8. "Yellow Fever in Cuba During the Spanish-American War." *The United States Army Yellow Fever Commission* website, (University of Virginia, Claude Moore Health Sciences Library). Updated July 28, 2015. http://exhibits .hsl.virginia.edu/yellowfever/

9. Ibid.

CHAPTER 7.   AMERICANS TURN TO SPAIN'S NEW WORLD ISLANDS

1. Virgil Carrington Jones, *Roosevelt's Rough Riders* (New York: Doubleday, 1971), p. 177.

2. Ibid., p. 179.

3. Graham A. Cosmas, *An Army for Empire* (Columbia: University of Missouri Press, 1971), p. 118.

4. Charles and Mary Beard, *The Rise of American Civilization* (New York: The Macmillan Company, 1934), vol. 2, pp. 159–161.

5. Cosmas, p. 166.

6. Wayne H. Morgan, *America's Road to Empire: The War With Spain and Overseas Expansion* (New York: John Wiley and Sons, Inc., 1965), p. 287.

CHAPTER 8.   OVERSEAS EMPIRE FOR AMERICA

1. Rodofo Sanchez, *La lucha larga de Cuba* (Mexico: Colegio de Mexico, 1954), p. 278.

2. Ibid., p. 283.

3. Edward Wilson, "Thank you Vasili Arkhipov, the man who stopped nuclear war." London, UK: *The Guardian*, October 27, 2012.

4. Ibid.

5. Wayne H. Morgan, *America's Road to Empire: The War With Spain and Overseas Expansion* (New York: John Wiley and Sons, Inc., 1965), p. 312.

6. Ibid., p. 313.

7. Ibid.

8. Joseph Smith, *The Spanish-American War* (New York: Longman Publishers, 1994), p. 197.

9. Ibid., p. 207.

10. Charles and Mary Beard, *The Rise of American Civilization* (New York: The Macmillan Company, 1934), vol. 2, p. 484.

11. Vincente L. Rafael, "Fagen, David (1875 - ?)" *BlackPast.org* Updated 2015. http://www.blackpast.org/aaw/fagen-david-1875.

12. Edmund Morris, *The Rise of Theodore Roosevelt* (New York: Ballantine Books, 1980), p. 665.

13. Louis Fisher, "Destruction of the Maine (1898)" *Law Library of Congress.* August 4, 2009. (Washington, DC: Library of Congress) http://www.loc.gov/law/help/usconlaw/pdf/Maine.1898.pdf

14. Smith, p. 292.

Glossary

battleship—A military warship with armor and large guns.

bituminous coal—A soft black rock burned as fossil fuel, which when newly broken will release more burnable gases in storage than the harder anthracite coal.

bombardment—The firing of many large guns at a target.

cable—An electronic message sent by telegraph cable.

collier—A person, or in the Navy a boat, for handling coal as fuel.

magazine—A room where ammunition is stored on board ship or in a military building.

mess kit—A portable set of cooking and eating tools used by soldiers, usually a knife, fork, and spoon in a metal pan with a handle.

mine—A bomb that can be triggered by contact.

one-pound gun—A large firearm which fires a shell weighing one pound (454 grams)

porthole—A round, sturdy window which can be fastened shut tightly, on board a ship.

quartermaster—A military officer who manages the supplies where military personnel are living.

regiment—A unit of soldiers, with two or more battle groups, leaders, and support.

revolution—The overthrow and complete replacement of an established government or political system.

squadron—A portion of a Naval fleet of ships, serving separately from the rest of the fleet.

tack or hardtack—A twice-baked dry biscuit carried as food for travelers or military personnel.

wound—An old-fashioned word for injury, particularly an injury during combat or military service.

For More Information

Books

Cherpak, Evelyn M., ed. *Three Splendid Little Wars: The Diary of Joseph K. Taussig*. Newport, RI: Naval War College Press, 2009.

Evans, Robley D. *A Sailor's Log: Recollections of Forty Years of Naval Life*. London, UK: Forgotten Books, 2015.

Golay, Michael. *Spanish-American War*. New York, NY: Chelsea House, 2010.

Jones, Gregg. *Honor in the Dust*. New York, NY: Penguin Group, 2012.

Offerman, Nick. *Gumption*. New York, NY: Dutton/Penguin Random House, 2015.

Steele, Matthew Forney. Walter H.T. Seager, ed. *The Spanish-American War*. North Charleston, SC: CreateSpace/Amazon OnDemand Publishing, 2014.

Websites

Cuban Battlefields of the Spanish-Cuban-American War, University of Nebraska
cubanbattlefields.unl.edu/background/about.php
Includes history, maps, and images related to the Spanish-American War.

"The Destruction of the USS *Maine*," **Naval Historical Center**
www.history.navy.mil/faqs/faq71-1.htm
Explores the destruction of the USS Maine.

The World of 1898: The Spanish-American War, Library of Congress
www.loc.gov/rr/hispanic/1898/index.html
Provides resources on the Spanish-American War, the events that led up to it, and the people involved.

Buffalo Soldier National Museum
buffalosoldiermuseum.com/
Information about the 9th and 10th cavalry and 24th and 25th infantry, the African-American Regiments in the US military

Videos

PBS/WGBH. "Crucible of Empire: The Spanish-American War." PBS Online. Posted 1999.
www.pbs.org/crucible/

History.com. Spanish-American War Videos.
www.history.com/topics/spanish-american-war/ videos

Index